The Wild Side

Beyond Belief

The Wild Side

Beyond Belief

Henry Billings

Melissa Billings

JAMESTOWN PUBLISHERS

a division of NTC/CONTEMPORARY PUBLISHING GROUP

Lincolnwood, Illinois USA

ISBN : 0-8092-9833-3

Published by Jamestown Publishers,
a division of NTC/Contemporary Publishing Group, Inc.
4255 West Touhy Avenue
Lincolnwood (Chicago), Illinois 60712-1975, U.S.A.
© 2001 NTC/Contemporary Publishing Group, all rights reserved.
No part of this publication may be reproduced, stored in a retrieval
system, or transmitted in any form or by any means without the
prior written permission of the publisher.

11 12 HES 12

CONTENTS

UNIT THREE

To the Student

We often hear about things that are difficult to believe. Sometimes they are miraculous stories. Sometimes they are terrible tragedies. Sometimes they are just events we can't explain.

The articles in this book are all about events that are hard to believe. Some of them are mysteries that have never been solved. Others are events that are very unusual. Some of them may have been caused by supernatural forces. You will probably learn something from every article. You will come away from many of them with unanswered questions. You may be intrigued or puzzled. You may be skeptical or amazed. But you will not be bored.

As you read and enjoy the 15 articles in this book, you will be developing your reading skills. If you complete all the lessons in this book, you will surely increase your reading speed and improve your reading comprehension and critical thinking skills. Also, because these exercises include items of the types often found on state and national tests, learning how to complete them will prepare you for tests you may have to take in the future.

How to Use This Book

About the Book. *Beyond Belief* contains three units, each of which includes five lessons. Each lesson begins with an article about an unusual subject or event. The article is followed by a group of four reading comprehension exercises and three critical thinking exercises. The reading comprehension exercises will help you understand the article. The critical thinking exercises will help you think about what you have read and how it relates to your own experience.

At the end of each lesson, you will also have the opportunity to give your personal response to some aspect of the article and then to assess how well you understood what you read.

The Sample Lesson. Working through the sample lesson, the first lesson in the book, with your class or group will demonstrate how a lesson is organized. The sample lesson explains how to complete the exercises and score your answers. The correct answers for the sample exercises and sample scores are printed in lighter type. In some cases, explanations of the correct answers are given. The explanations will help you understand how to think through these question types.

If you have any questions about how to complete the exercises or score them, this is the time to get the answers.

Working Through Each Lesson. Begin each lesson by looking at the photograph and reading the caption. Before you read, predict what you think the article will be about. Then read the article.

Sometimes your teacher may decide to time your reading. Timing helps you keep track of and increase your reading speed. If you have been timed, enter your reading time in the box at the end of the lesson. Then use the Words-per-Minute Table to find your reading speed, and record your speed on the Reading Speed graph at the end of the unit.

Next complete the Reading Comprehension and Critical Thinking exercises. The directions for each exercise will tell you how to mark your answers. When you have finished all four Reading Comprehension exercises, use the answer key provided by your teacher to check your work. Follow the directions after each exercise to find your score. Record your Reading Comprehension scores on the graph at the end of each unit. Then check your answers to the Author's Approach, Summarizing and Paraphrasing, and Critical Thinking exercises. Fill in the Critical Thinking chart at the end of each unit with your evaluation of your work and comments about your progress.

At the end of each unit you will also complete a Compare and Contrast chart. The completed chart will help you see what the articles have in common, and it will give you an opportunity to explore your own ideas about the events in the articles.

SAMPLE LESSON

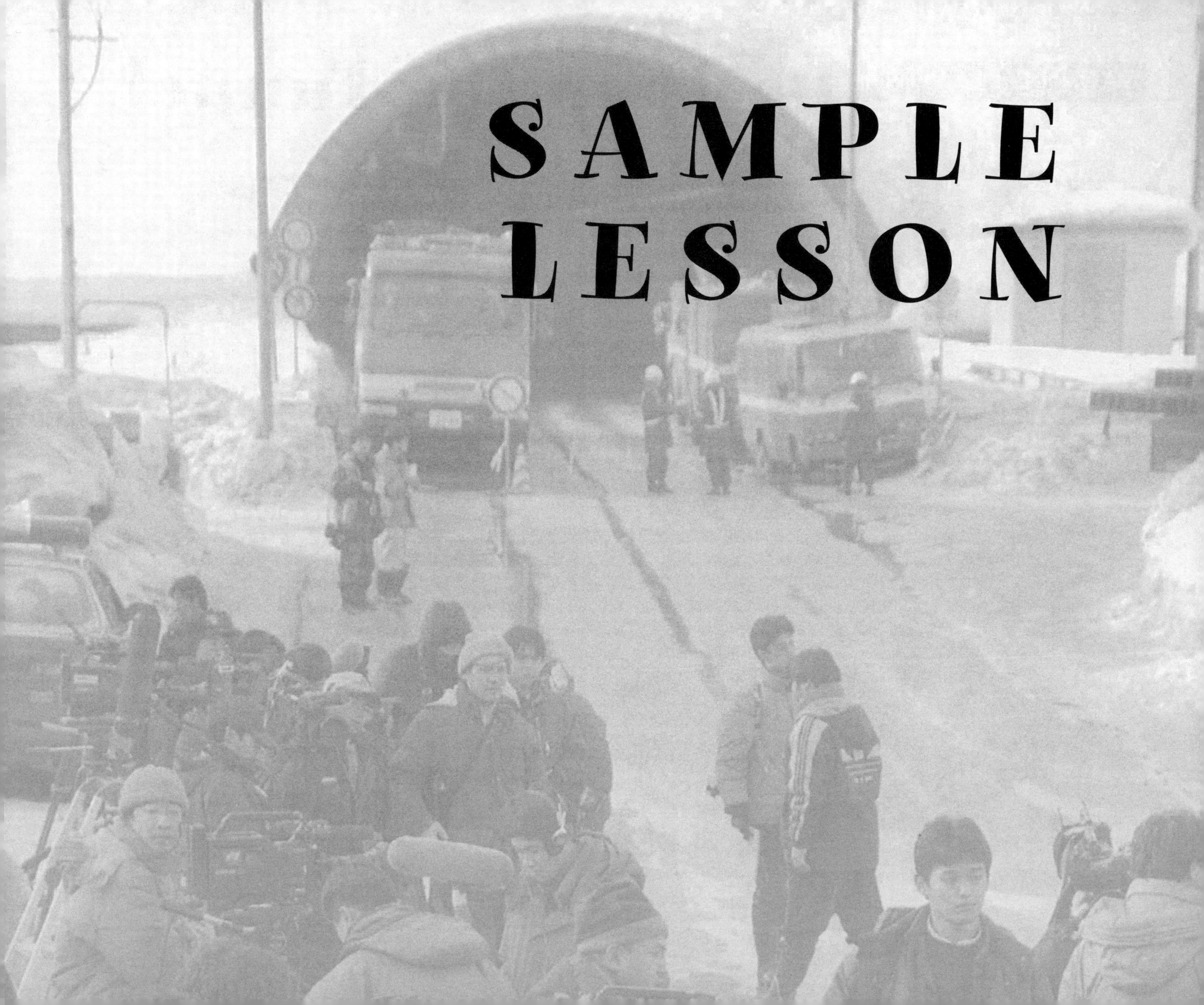

Death in the Tunnel

¹Falling Rocks!

² Anyone who has driven through a mountain region has read a road sign like this one. Most people don't even notice such signs. If they do, they don't give them much thought. After all, what are the odds of being killed by a rock as it falls down a mountain?

³ If you think those odds are long, what would you say are the chances of being killed by a falling rock while driving through a tunnel? Believe it or not, it has happened. On February 10, 1996, a huge rock broke free from a mountain on the Japanese island of Hokkaido. It fell right onto the Toyohama Tunnel.

Japanese media gather in front of the entrance to the Toyohama Tunnel shortly after the boulder fell.

⁴ The rock that fell wasn't just a rock. It was a boulder. It weighed close to 50,000 tons. It was 210 feet tall and 120 feet wide. That made it as big as a 20-story building.

⁵ The falling boulder hit the top of the Toyohama Tunnel and crashed right through. At that exact moment, a car was passing through the tunnel. So was a bus carrying 19 people. About half of the people on the bus were teenagers. They came from the nearby fishing village of Furubira. They were on their way to a winter carnival. Both the bus and the car were pinned underneath the huge boulder.

⁶ No one knows for sure why the boulder broke free. Perhaps a small earthquake had loosened it. There are many earthquakes in that part of Japan. Or perhaps the weather was to blame. It often snows in Hokkaido. When the snow melts, the water runs into cracks in the mountains. Then cold weather comes again, turning the water to ice. As the water becomes ice, it expands. It does so with enough force to crack a rock. Over many years, the ice could have opened a bigger and bigger crack in the

mountain. In time, the ice could have loosened a boulder.

⁷ This was not the first massive boulder to fall in Hokkaido. Eighteen months earlier a boulder had fallen. It hit the ground not far from the Toyohama Tunnel. That boulder was twice as big as this one. Luckily, though, that one did not fall on anyone.

⁸ This time, 20 people were trapped under the boulder. Were any of them still alive? Rescuers managed to slip a tiny camera down through the debris into the tunnel. The camera showed parts of the crushed car and bus. It picked up no signs of life. But there was still the possibility that someone had survived. They had to get into the tunnel to find out. Everyone agreed it had to be done, but no one knew quite how to do it.

⁹ For 11 long hours, rescuers talked about what to do. At last, they decided not to dig straight through the tunnel. That would weaken the land above the tunnel's roof. Then they might have a second rockfall on their hands. Instead, they decided they would try to move the huge

boulder. Then they could dig in through the top of the tunnel.

10   Meanwhile, friends and family members of the victims rushed to the site. There they waited for news. Soon it began to snow. The temperature fell quickly. "Hurry up! Please hurry up!" cried some of the people to the rescuers. They knew that if the rescuers didn't get into the tunnel soon, anyone still alive would freeze to death.

11   The rescuers decided to blast the boulder off the roof. With enough force, they could blow it into the sea below the tunnel. So they set off 550 pounds of dynamite. It was not enough. Only a tiny piece of the boulder broke off.

12   The rescuers could have used more dynamite. But they feared that too big a blast would cause a second rockfall. "We did not achieve our aim of removing the boulder because we cut the amount [of dynamite] for safety reasons," said one rescuer.

13   The next day, rescuers tried another blast. But again, only a small piece of the boulder broke off. The following day they tried a third time. Still, they couldn't topple the rock. By this time,

three days had passed. Family members and friends began to lose hope. "The past few days I've cried and cried while watching this unfold," said one relative. "I just don't have any more tears."

14   Some of the people became angry. They figured their loved ones inside the tunnel were dead by this time. All they wanted was to retrieve the bodies. "Even if they are dead, hurry up and pull them out of there," one person demanded.

15   On the fourth day, the rescuers blasted the boulder again. This time it worked. The explosion sent the boulder plunging down into the sea below the tunnel.

16   Even with the boulder gone, there was still a lot of work to do. The roof of the tunnel itself had to be cleared away. That took another two days. At last, on February 16, the rescuers reached the car. It had taken a direct hit. The force of the falling boulder was so enormous it drove the car into the ground. The driver, a 20-year-old clerk, was found dead at the wheel.

17   The day after that, rescuers finally reached the bus. It, too, had taken a direct hit. The bus had been crushed

to a height of just three feet. No one inside was alive. Family members took some comfort in learning that the passengers had died right away. In that sense, the delay in digging out the tunnel had not mattered.

18   Villagers from Furubira later put up an altar at the tunnel. It was meant to honor the dead. But it also served as a warning. A sign that reads Falling Rocks should be taken seriously. While the odds against it are great, rocks perched high above the road can break loose and kill people.

If you have been timed while reading this article, enter your reading time below. Then turn to the Words-per-Minute Table on page 55 and look up your reading speed (words per minute). Enter your reading speed on the graph on page 56.

Reading Time: Sample Lesson

————— : —————
Minutes   *Seconds*

A | Finding the Main Idea

One statement below expresses the main idea of the article. One statement is too general, or too broad. The other statement explains only part of the article; it is too narrow. Label the statements using the following key:

M—Main Idea   **B—Too Broad**   **N—Too Narrow**

___B___ 1. Hokkaido, Japan, has many earthquakes, which often cause rockfalls. [This statement is true, but it is *too broad.* Japan does have many earthquakes that cause rockfalls, but this article talks about a specific rockfall.]

___N___ 2. The boulder that fell on the Toyohama Tunnel was as big as a 20-story building. [This statement is true, but it is *too narrow.* The boulder was as big as a 20-story building, but the article focuses more on the efforts to remove the boulder.]

___M___ 3. In 1996, a boulder fell on Toyohama Tunnel in Japan, killing the 20 people who were driving through the tunnel at the time. [This statement is the *main idea.* It tells you what the selection is about.]

___15___ Score 15 points for a correct M answer.

___10___ Score 5 points for each correct B or N answer.

___25___ **Total Score:** Finding the Main Idea

B | Recalling Facts

How well do you remember the facts in the article? Put an X in the box next to the answer that correctly completes each statement about the article.

1. When the boulder fell, a bus full of teenagers was in the tunnel on the way to
   □ a. Furubira.
   □ b. Hokkaido.
   ☒ c. a winter carnival.

2. A possible explanation of what caused the boulder to fall is
   ☒ a. an earthquake.
   □ b. an explosion.
   □ c. a blizzard.

3. The rescuers used a small amount of dynamite to move the boulder because they
   ☒ a. didn't want to cause a second rockfall.
   □ b. didn't want to hurt the people inside the tunnel.
   □ c. thought it would be enough to move the boulder.

4. Some people became angry with the rescuers because
   □ a. their loved ones had died.
   □ b. they didn't want to move the boulder.
   ☒ c. it took a long time to clear the tunnel.

5. When the rescuers finally reached the bus, they discovered that
   ☒ a. all the passengers had died instantly.
   □ b. some passengers had frozen to death.
   □ c. all the passengers were from Furubira.

Score 5 points for each correct answer.

___25___ **Total Score:** Recalling Facts

C | Making Inferences

When you combine your own experience with information from a text to draw a conclusion that is not directly stated in that text, you are making an inference. Below are five statements that may or may not be inferences based on information in the article. Label the statements using the following key:

C—Correct Inference   F—Faulty Inference

___F___ 1. Boulders fall often in Hokkaido, Japan. [This is a *faulty* inference. The article mentions two boulders that fell in Hokkaido, but that does not imply that boulders fall often.]

___C___ 2. The rescuers wanted to be sure they were doing the right thing. [This is a *correct* inference. The article states that the rescuers talked about what to do for 11 hours before doing anything, and that they did not use more dynamite than they thought was safe.]

___C___ 3. It is not safe to have several dynamite blasts in one spot during one day. [This is a *correct* inference. You can infer that the rescuers would have done more dynamite blasts per day if that were safe.]

___C___ 4. The victims' family and friends thought the rescuers were working too slowly. [This is a *correct* inference. The article mentions several angry comments made by relatives of the victims about the speed of the rescue operation.]

___F___ 5. Some of the victims would have survived if the rescuers had acted more quickly. [This is a *faulty* inference. The article states that all of the victims died immediately.]

Score 5 points for each correct answer.

___25___ **Total Score:** Making Inferences

D | Using Words Precisely

Each numbered sentence below contains an underlined word or phrase from the article. Following the sentence are three definitions. One definition is closest to the meaning of the underlined word. One definition is opposite or nearly opposite. Label those two definitions using the following key; do not label the remaining definition.

C—Closest   O—Opposite or Nearly Opposite

1. Both the bus and the car were <u>pinned</u> underneath the huge boulder.

___C___ a. held down

_____ b. crushed

___O___ c. free to move

2. As the water becomes ice, it <u>expands</u>.

_____ a. melts

___C___ b. grows larger

___O___ c. grows smaller

3. This was not the first <u>massive</u> boulder to fall in Hokkaido.

___C___ a. huge

_____ b. heavy

___O___ c. small

4. Still, they couldn't <u>topple</u> the rock.

___O___ a. hold up

___C___ b. knock down

_____ c. throw

5. All they wanted was to <u>retrieve</u> the bodies.

____O____ a. leave

_____ b. find

____C____ c. rescue

____15____ Score 3 points for each correct C answer.

____10____ Score 2 points for each correct O answer.

____25____ **Total Score:** Using Words Precisely

Enter the four total scores in the spaces below, and add them together to find your Reading Comprehension Score. Then record your Reading Comprehension Score on the graph on page 57.

Score	Question Type	Sample Lesson
25	Finding the Main Idea	
25	Recalling Facts	
25	Making Inferences	
25	Using Words Precisely	
100	**Reading Comprehension Score**	

Author's Approach

Put an X in the box next to the correct answer.

1. What is the authors' purpose in writing "Death in the Tunnel"?

☒ a. to describe what happened at the Toyohama Tunnel in February 1996

☐ b. to inform readers about the danger of falling rocks

☐ c. to convince people to be more careful when driving through tunnels

2. The authors use the first sentence of the article to

☐ a. describe the setting of the article.

☐ b. emphasize the danger of falling rocks.

☒ c. get the reader's attention.

3. The authors tell this story mainly by

☐ a. using their imagination and creativity.

☒ b. describing the events chronologically.

☐ c. retelling the experiences of different people in the article.

____3____ Number of correct answers

Record your personal assessment of your work on the Critical Thinking Chart on page 58.

Summarizing and Paraphrasing

Follow the directions provided for question 1. Put an X in the box next to the correct answer for questions 2 and 3.

1. Look for the important ideas and events in paragraphs 4 and 5. Summarize those paragraphs in one or two sentences.

   [Explain the main ideas in these paragraphs.]

   _____

   _____

2. Below are summaries of the article. Choose the summary that says the most important things about the article but in the fewest words.

   ☐ a. It took rescuers a long time to find the bodies of the people who had been crushed in the Toyohama Tunnel in Japan. [This summary omits information about how the people were crushed.]

   ☒ b. A boulder fell on the Toyohama Tunnel in Japan in February 1996, killing 20 people. It took rescuers seven days to remove the boulder and reach the bodies of the victims. [This summary states all the important ideas in the article without too many unnecessary details.]

   ☐ c. A huge boulder fell on the Toyohama Tunnel in Japan in February 1996. 20 people were in the tunnel at the time, including a bus full of people on their way to a winter festival. It took rescuers seven days to remove the boulder and find the victims. All of them had died right away. [This summary includes figures and information about the people in the tunnel, which are not necessary for a summary.]

3. Choose the sentence that correctly restates the following sentence from the article: "The explosion sent the boulder plunging down into the sea below the tunnel."

   ☒ a. After the explosion, the boulder fell into the sea. [This is the *correct* paraphrase. It restates the ideas in the original statement.]

   ☐ b. The boulder rolled off the tunnel into the sea. [This sentence is an *incorrect* paraphrase; it does not state what caused the boulder to fall off the tunnel, which is stated in the original sentence.]

   ☐ c. The boulder fell off the tunnel into the sea, causing an explosion. [This sentence is an *incorrect* paraphrase; the explosion caused the boulder to fall, not the other way around.]

   > ___3___ Number of correct answers
   >
   > Record your personal assessment of your work on the Critical Thinking Chart on page 58.

Critical Thinking

Put an X in the box next to the correct answer for question 1. Follow the directions provided for the other questions.

1. Which of the following statements from the article is an opinion rather than a fact?

   ☐ a. It weighed close to 50,000 tons.

   ☒ b. In time, the ice could have loosened a boulder.

   ☐ c. At last, on February 16, the rescuers reached the car.

2. Choose from the letters below to correctly complete the following statement. Write the letters on the lines.

   On the negative side, ___b___, but on the positive side ___c___.

   a. people were upset that the rescue effort took so long

   b. all of the people who were in the tunnel when the boulder fell were killed

   c. they all died instantly

3. Which paragraphs provide evidence from the article to support your answer to question 2?

   ___[paragraphs 16 & 17]___

4. Choose from the letters below to correctly complete the following statement. Write the letters on the lines.

   According to the article, ___c___ may have caused a huge boulder to ___a___, and the effect was that ___b___.

   a. fall on the Toyohama Tunnel

   b. 20 people were killed

   c. snowy weather

   ___5___ Number of correct answers

   Record your personal assessment of your work on the Critical Thinking Chart on page 58.

Personal Response

I can't believe

___[Write something you found hard to believe while reading___

___the article.]___

_____

_____

Self-Assessment

From reading this article, I have learned

___[Write something you learned while reading the article.]___

_____

_____

_____

Self-Assessment

To get the most out of the *Wild Side* series program, you need to take charge of your own progress in improving your reading comprehension and critical thinking skills. Here are some of the features that help you work on those essential skills.

Reading Comprehension Exercises. Complete these exercises immediately after reading each article. They help you recall what you have read, understand the stated and implied main ideas, and add words to your working vocabulary.

Critical Thinking Skills Exercises. These exercises help you focus on the author's approach and purpose, recognize and generate summaries and paraphrases, and identify relationships between ideas.

Personal Response and Self-Assessment. Questions in this category help you relate the articles to your personal experience and give you the opportunity to evaluate your understanding of the information in that lesson.

Compare and Contrast Charts. At the end of each unit you will complete a Compare and Contrast chart. The completed chart helps you see what the articles have in common and gives you an opportunity to explore your own ideas about the topics discussed in the articles.

The Graphs. The graphs and charts at the end of each unit enable you to keep track of your progress. Check your graphs regularly with your teacher. Decide whether your progress is satisfactory or whether you need additional work on some skills. What types of exercises are you having difficulty with? Talk with your teacher about ways to work on the skills in which you need the most practice.

UNIT ONE

A Graveyard Mystery

SPITZ

DESIREE A.
1874–1978

HENRY
1880–1916

HARRY SPITZ
JULY 9, 1909
SEPT 8, 1912

[1] Harry Spitz seemed like an ordinary little boy. He had his father's looks, with blond hair and brown eyes. He liked to laugh and play with his toys. But was Harry really just an ordinary child? That's the question people began to ask in July 1975. By then, Harry had been dead for 63 years. But something happened that summer that made everyone remember him. It made them think perhaps there was more to the little boy than met the eye.

[2] Harry Spitz was born in 1909. He lived with his parents in Morgantown, West Virginia. There his father worked

Harry Spitz's grave, shown here as it looks today, is located next to his parents' graves. Harry's vault popped out of the ground on this same spot in 1975.

in a glass factory. The family did not have a lot of money. Still, by all accounts, Harry was a happy child. When he was three years old, though, tragedy struck. Harry came down with cholera, a deadly disease. Eight days after catching the disease, he died.

[3] Harry's parents were crushed. With heavy hearts they made arrangements for the funeral. His body was dressed in a blue and white outfit. Flowers were placed in his hands. His favorite toy—a little stuffed lion—was put into the casket with him. The Spitzes had two engraved plaques made for the casket. Each read Our Darling. One went inside the casket. The second one was set on top.

[4] Many of Harry's playmates came to the funeral. Afterwards a horse-drawn carriage took the casket to Oak Grove Cemetery. There an open grave lay waiting. Several feet down was a concrete vault. The casket was lowered into the vault. The engraved plaque was placed on top of the casket. Someone laid a single flower on it. Then workers sealed the vault with a three-inch-thick concrete lid. They shoveled several feet of dirt on top of

the vault to fill up the grave.

[5] Everyone thought that was the end of Harry Spitz. And for 63 years, it was. But on July 2, 1975, Harry was back in the news. That morning the caretaker of Oak Grove Cemetery saw a small pile of dirt near Harry's tombstone. Walking closer, he saw a bizarre sight. The ground over Harry's grave had buckled. The burial vault was poking up through the grass. The caretaker could see that a corner of the vault had split open, and the lid was resting at an angle. It didn't look like someone had dug up the vault. All the earth had been pushed up from underneath the ground.

[6] The caretaker wasn't sure what to think. He wondered if some kids had set off fireworks near the grave. Perhaps one backfired and ruptured the grave. In any case, he called the police. Chief Bennie Palmer and Officer Ralph Chapman took the call. Before seeing the grave, Palmer thought he knew what had happened. From time to time a strange group of people gathered in the cemetery. They tried to make contact with the spirits of dead people. He figured the group

had come again in the night. He suspected they had set off some kind of explosive device.

7   When Palmer checked out Harry's grave, however, he changed his mind. "There was no evidence of such a device," he said. In fact, there was no sign of an explosion at all. "We didn't find any evidence of charred earth or gunpowder residues."

8   Next Palmer wondered if there was a natural gas leak in the area. Perhaps that could have blown the vault up out of the ground. He called the gas company and asked them to check. Workers did check, but found no leaks.

9   Palmer and Chapman could not think of anything else that would have caused the vault to pop out of the ground. Yet that's what it had done. Clearly no one had dug up the grave. There was not a single spot where anything had cut into the ground. "It was a real mystery," Chapman said. "There just weren't any signs of tampering from the outside."

10   For the next few days many people tried to figure out what had caused Harry Spitz's grave to open. Scientists and professors were consulted. None of them had any answers. There had been no earthquakes or tremors in the region. There had been no build-up of gases in the ground or in the vault. As Chief Palmer said, "It was really baffling."

11   At last officials decided to open the vault and take out the casket. Harry's body needed to be reburied anyway. When the lid was removed from the vault, the mystery just got deeper. The engraved plaque was still perched on top of the rounded casket. So was the single dried flower. This meant no explosion could possibly have pushed the vault up through the ground. Anything that shook the vault that much would have caused the plaque and flower to fall off.

12   The case was already an eerie one. But it got even spookier when workers opened the casket. Harry's body was indeed lying inside. But it did not look like it had been there for 63 years. "The body . . . was not in the bare-bones state, which it should have been after all that time," said Chapman. Everyone had expected to see little more than a skeleton. Instead, they saw a little boy who looked like he was sleeping. His hands still held a bouquet of dried flowers. "The body still had intact skin," said Chapman. That skin was a little leathery, but everything else about Harry was in remarkably good shape. "He even had lots of long blond hair."

13   No one could explain it. But many people were a bit frightened by it. They wondered what it all meant. They wondered what forces had been at work in the grave. And they wished they knew more about the little boy who was buried there.

14   On July 12, 1975, Harry Spitz's body was buried for a second time. His casket was put into a new, sealed vault. Since then the vault has remained where it belongs—deep in the ground. But no one knows how much longer it will stay that way.

If you have been timed while reading this article, enter your reading time below. Then turn to the Words-per-Minute Table on page 55 and look up your reading speed (words per minute). Enter your reading speed on the graph on page 56.

Reading Time: Lesson 1

_____ : _____
Minutes   Seconds

A Finding the Main Idea

One statement below expresses the main idea of the article. One statement is too general, or too broad. The other statement explains only part of the article; it is too narrow. Label the statements using the following key:

M—Main Idea   B—Too Broad   N—Too Narrow

_____ 1. It remains a mystery why young Harry Spitz's vault popped up from the ground with his body still intact 63 years after his death.

_____ 2. In 1975 people began to wonder if Harry Spitz had been just an ordinary little boy.

_____ 3. When officials opened the vault of Harry Spitz's grave, they realized an explosion could not have pushed it through the ground.

_____ Score 15 points for a correct M answer.

_____ Score 5 points for each correct B or N answer.

_____ **Total Score:** Finding the Main Idea

B Recalling Facts

How well do you remember the facts in the article? Put an X in the box next to the answer that correctly completes each statement about the article.

1. When Harry Spitz's body was buried for the first time,
   - ☐ a. a single flower was laid in his hands.
   - ☐ b. an engraved plaque was attached to the casket.
   - ☐ c. a stuffed lion was buried with him.

2. On July 2, 1975, the caretaker at Oak Grove Cemetery saw
   - ☐ a. Harry Spitz's body poking through the ground.
   - ☐ b. Harry Spitz's burial vault poking through the ground.
   - ☐ c. fireworks near Harry Spitz's grave.

3. One theory the policemen had about Harry's grave was that
   - ☐ a. there was a natural gas leak in the area.
   - ☐ b. someone had set off fireworks near the grave.
   - ☐ c. someone had dug up the vault.

4. When Harry Spitz's casket was opened,
   - ☐ a. the body was in remarkably good shape.
   - ☐ b. the little boy was sleeping.
   - ☐ c. only bones were found.

5. On July 12, 1975,
   - ☐ a. Harry Spitz's vault popped out of the ground a second time.
   - ☐ b. Harry Spitz's body was buried for a second time.
   - ☐ c. Harry Spitz's casket was sealed.

Score 5 points for each correct answer.

_____ **Total Score:** Recalling Facts

C Making Inferences

When you combine your own experience with information from a text to draw a conclusion that is not directly stated in that text, you are making an inference. Below are five statements that may or may not be inferences based on information in the article. Label the statements using the following key:

C—Correct Inference   F—Faulty Inference

_____ 1. Harry was well-loved by his family and friends.

_____ 2. Natural forces disturbed Harry's grave.

_____ 3. It is unlikely that anyone will ever know what caused Harry Spitz's vault to pop out of the ground.

_____ 4. Harry Spitz was buried alive.

_____ 5. Harry Spitz had supernatural powers.

Score 5 points for each correct answer.

_____ **Total Score:** Making Inferences

D Using Words Precisely

Each numbered sentence below contains an underlined word or phrase from the article. Following the sentence are three definitions. One definition is closest to the meaning of the underlined word. One definition is opposite or nearly opposite. Label those two definitions using the following key; do not label the remaining definition.

C—Closest   O—Opposite or Nearly Opposite

1. His parents were <u>crushed</u>.

_____ a. very sad

_____ b. worried

_____ c. overjoyed

2. The ground over Harry's grave had <u>buckled</u>.

_____ a. remained unbroken

_____ b. been moved

_____ c. collapsed

3. There just weren't any signs of <u>tampering</u> from the outside.

_____ a. disturbance

_____ b. ignoring

_____ c. digging

4. It was really <u>baffling</u>.

_____ a. clear

_____ b. frightening

_____ c. puzzling

5. The body still had <u>intact</u> skin.

_____ a. destroyed

_____ b. attached

_____ c. removed

_____ Score 3 points for each correct C answer.

_____ Score 2 points for each correct O answer.

_____ **Total Score:** Using Words Precisely

Enter the four total scores in the spaces below, and add them together to find your Reading Comprehension Score. Then record your Reading Comprehension Score on the graph on page 57.

Score	Question Type	Lesson 1
_____	Finding the Main Idea	
_____	Recalling Facts	
_____	Making Inferences	
_____	Using Words Precisely	
_____	**Reading Comprehension Score**	

Author's Approach

Put an X in the box next to the correct answer.

1. What do the authors imply by saying, "Harry Spitz seemed like an ordinary little boy"?

☐ a. Harry Spitz was not an ordinary little boy.

☐ b. Harry Spitz was like other little boys.

☐ c. Harry Spitz was not an interesting boy.

2. Based on the information in the article, you can conclude that the authors want you to think that

☐ a. Harry Spitz's burial vault might pop up from the ground again.

☐ b. Harry Spitz is not really dead.

☐ c. Harry Spitz had something to do with his own burial vault popping up from the ground.

3. Which of the following statements from the article best describes how the people of Morgantown felt about Harry Spitz's grave?

☐ a. Police Chief Palmer thought he knew what had happened.

☐ b. Clearly no one had dug up the grave.

☐ c. "It was really baffling."

_____ Number of correct answers

Record your personal assessment of your work on the Critical Thinking Chart on page 58.

Summarizing and Paraphrasing

Follow the directions provided for question 1. Put an X in the box next to the correct answer for the other questions.

1. Reread paragraph 2 in the article. Below, write a summary of the paragraph in no more than 25 words.

_____

_____

_____

_____

Reread your summary and decide whether it covers the important ideas in the paragraph. Next, decide how to shorten the summary to 15 words or less without leaving out any essential information. Write this summary below.

_____

_____

_____

2. Choose the sentence that correctly restates the following sentence from the article: "Since then, the vault has remained where it belongs—deep in the ground."

☐ a. The vault has not moved since then.

☐ b. The vault is in the ground.

☐ c. The vault belongs in the ground.

3. Below are summaries of the article. Choose the summary that says all the most important things about the article in the fewest words.

☐ a. No one has figured out why the vault containing Harry Spitz's casket popped out of the ground and his body was found nearly intact 63 years after his death.

☐ b. Harry Spitz died when he was three years old, and 63 years later the vault he was buried in mysteriously popped out of the ground. When investigators opened the casket, they found his body nearly intact, even his hair. To this day, no one has been able to explain this mystery.

☐ c. The vault containing Harry Spitz's casket popped out of the ground, and no one could explain why.

_____ Number of correct answers

Record your personal assessment of your work on the Critical Thinking Chart on page 58.

Critical Thinking

Put an X in the box next to the correct answer for questions 1–3. Follow the directions provided for questions 4 and 5.

1. Which of the following statements from the article is an opinion rather than a fact?

☐ a. Harry Spitz was born in 1909.

☐ b. No one knows how much longer [the grave] will stay [in the ground].

☐ c. The ground over Harry's grave had buckled.

2. Into which of the following theme categories would this story best fit?

☐ a. mystery

☐ b. science fiction

☐ c. drama

3. What was the effect of opening Harry Spitz's casket?

☐ a. The officials working on the case were frightened.

☐ b. The mystery got even deeper.

☐ c. Harry's body had not decayed.

4. Choose from the letters below to correctly complete the following statement. Write the letters on the lines.

According to paragraph 11, _____ because _____ .

☐ a. Harry's body needed to be reburied anyway

☐ b. no explosion could have pushed the vault up through the ground

☐ c. officials opened the vault

5. Which paragraphs provide evidence from the article that support your answer to question 4?

_____

_____

_____ Number of correct answers
Record your personal assessment of your work on the Critical Thinking Chart on page 58.

Personal Response

How do you think you would have felt if you had found Harry Spitz's vault poking up through the ground?

_____

_____

_____

_____

Self-Assessment

I can't really understand how

_____

_____

_____

_____

The Money Pit

This photograph of the Money Pit was taken in 1955 during one of the many unsuccessful attempts to reach the bottom.

¹In the year 1795, a teenager named Dan McGinnis paddled his canoe to Oak Island. At that time no one lived on the small island off the coast of Nova Scotia. So it was a fine spot for a young boy to hunt. But McGinnis did not do much hunting that day. Instead, he found something that has puzzled the people of Canada ever since.

² While resting under a tree, McGinnis saw a round depression in the ground. He also spotted a notch in one of the tree's branches. It looked as if the branch had been used as part of a pulley. McGinnis's mind began to

race. He had heard tales of pirates in the region. Had pirates buried treasure under this tree?

3   The next day McGinnis returned to the island with two friends. They began to dig. The boys dug only a few feet when they hit something hard. It was a layer of flagstones. There *was* something buried here!

4   The boys dug faster and faster. At 10 feet they ran into a layer of wooden planks. They hoped that there was treasure buried under the planks, but there wasn't. There was just more dirt. Still, they figured someone had put the planks there for a reason. There had to be treasure somewhere in the pit. They just had to dig deeper.

5   Day after day the boys returned to the deserted island. At 20 feet, they hit another layer of planks. Excitedly, they lifted them up. But again, all they found was more dirt. They resumed digging.

6   At 30 feet they hit a third layer of wooden planks. Again, there was nothing underneath but more dirt. By this time winter was coming. The boys couldn't dig any more. But they vowed to return to the island in the

future and uncover the treasure. They were sure something important was buried there. Why else would anyone have built such an elaborate pit?

7   The boys dug on and off for the next few years without reaching the bottom of the pit. They grew to be adults. Still, they dreamed of finding treasure in what became known as the Money Pit. In 1804 they joined a company formed solely to find the treasure. With better tools, they could now dig deeper.

8   But even with the new tools, it was the same story all over again. Every 10 feet, the workers hit a layer of oak planks. Under every layer of planks there was more dirt. They did get a few thrills, however. At 40 feet they found a layer of charcoal on top of the planks. At 50 feet there was a layer of putty like the kind used to seal ships. Ten more feet, and they dug up coconut fibers. At last, at 90 feet, they found a stone marked with strange writing.

9   They began to get excited when they found the stone. This had to be it! The next day the workers returned, brimming with hope. But one look

down into the Money Pit deflated all their dreams. The pit had flooded overnight. It was filled with water all the way up to the 33-foot level. No amount of bailing with buckets or pumping could empty the pit.

10   As it turned out, this was a booby trap. Whoever built the Money Pit wanted to keep outsiders away. So a tunnel had been created that led from the pit to the ocean. The digging had opened that tunnel. That meant that water flowed freely from the ocean into the pit.

11   McGinnis and his friends were frustrated. But they weren't ready to give up yet. If they couldn't dig any further into the Money Pit, they reasoned, then they would dig a second pit right next to it. When they were deep enough, they would cut over to the Money Pit and grab the treasure.

12   The workers dug a 110-foot shaft. But when they started to cut over, water rushed into the new shaft as well. They had to scramble to escape with their lives. Soon the second shaft had just as much water in it as the Money Pit. All McGinnis and the

others had to show for their work was two holes filled with water.

13 For years after that, the Money Pit lay untouched. But in 1849 a new group came to the island. Calling themselves the Truro Company, they vowed to solve the mystery. They brought in the most up-to-date mining equipment they could find. Then they drilled down and collected samples of whatever lay at the bottom of the pit. They came up with pieces of oak, spruce, and metal. These clues suggested the drill had hit chests filled with coins. They also found three small gold links from a chain. But there was no way to get at the treasure. No matter what they did, water always filled the pit.

14 Over the years other people have tried their luck. Some have built more shafts. (In fact, people have built so many shafts that no one now knows which one is the original Money Pit.) They have built dams to try to stop the flooding. They have tried better pumps. But nothing has worked. No one has ever found any coins or gold.

15 Millions of dollars have been spent trying to find the treasure. There have been human costs as well. Treasure hunters have been killed in the Money Pit. One man died when a water boiler blew up. Another fell to his death while being pulled up from the bottom of the pit. In 1965, a father, his son, and two friends drowned in the pit.

16 The Money Pit has remained a mystery for over 200 years. To this day, no one knows if there is treasure buried there, or why such an elaborate pit was built in the first place. But there is another mystery, as well: Who built the pit? Dan McGinnis thought the builders were pirates. But that is not likely. Whoever built the pit had to be an engineer with a team of skilled miners. No known pirate had the skill or support to construct such a pit.

17 Rupert Furneaux, author of *The Money Pit Mystery*, may have a better answer. He thinks gold was buried on Oak Island during the American Revolution. The British governor of New York had the gold to pay all of the British forces in America. In 1778 it looked like the Americans might capture New York City. So perhaps the governor sent the money to Nova Scotia to be buried. The British army would have had the right skills to build the pit.

18 There is a problem with this theory, however. There is no record that the British lost a huge sum of money during that time. Furneaux thinks he can explain that too. He believes the British dug up the money themselves soon after hiding it. He thinks the pit is just that—a pit.

19 Maybe Furneaux is right. Maybe there is nothing in the Money Pit but water and broken dreams. On the other hand, no one has explained how the British could have gotten the treasure out of the pit. And no one has explained why bits of gold, metal, and wood would still be in the bottom of the pit. So maybe there *are* chests of gold down there. Maybe they are just waiting for someone to pull them out. Could that someone be you?

If you have been timed while reading this article, enter your reading time below. Then turn to the Words-per-Minute Table on page 55 and look up your reading speed (words per minute). Enter your reading speed on the graph on page 56.

Reading Time: Lesson 2

_____ : _____
Minutes   Seconds

A Finding the Main Idea

One statement below expresses the main idea of the article. One statement is too general, or too broad. The other statement explains only part of the article; it is too narrow. Label the statements using the following key:

M—Main Idea   **B—Too Broad**   **N—Too Narrow**

_____ 1. Tunnels that let water into the pit have kept treasure hunters from discovering what is at the bottom of the Money Pit.

_____ 2. Many people wonder if there is treasure buried in the Money Pit.

_____ 3. Although many people have tried to find out what lies at the bottom of the Money Pit, its contents remain a mystery.

_____ Score 15 points for a correct M answer.

_____ Score 5 points for each correct B or N answer.

_____ **Total Score:** Finding the Main Idea

B Recalling Facts

How well do you remember the facts in the article? Put an X in the box next to the answer that correctly completes each statement about the article.

1. While he was resting under a tree on Oak Island in 1795, Dan McGinnis noticed
   ☐ a. a pulley attached to a tree.
   ☐ b. a round depression in the ground.
   ☐ c. wooden planks in the ground.

2. The first thing McGinnis and his friends found in the Money Pit was
   ☐ a. a layer of wooden planks.
   ☐ b. a layer of flagstones.
   ☐ c. gold links from a chain.

3. The water that filled the pit came from
   ☐ a. an underground river.
   ☐ b. a pipe.
   ☐ c. the ocean.

4. When workers drilled to the bottom of the pit, they found
   ☐ a. gold coins.
   ☐ b. gold links from a chain.
   ☐ c. an oak chest.

5. Author Rupert Furneaux believes the Money Pit was constructed during the American Revolution by
   ☐ a. the British governor of New York.
   ☐ b. American soldiers.
   ☐ c. British soldiers.

Score 5 points for each correct answer.

_____ **Total Score:** Recalling Facts

C | Making Inferences

When you combine your own experience with information from a text to draw a conclusion that is not directly stated in that text, you are making an inference. Below are five statements that may or may not be inferences based on information in the article. Label the statements using the following key:

C—Correct Inference   F—Faulty Inference

_____ 1. Dan McGinnis never lost hope of finding treasure in the Money Pit.

_____ 2. The people who built the Money Pit were rich.

_____ 3. There are chests full of coins in the bottom of the Money Pit.

_____ 4. The designer of the Money Pit was a clever engineer.

_____ 5. Many people are captivated by the idea of finding buried treasure.

Score 5 points for each correct answer.

_____ **Total Score:** Making Inferences

D | Using Words Precisely

Each numbered sentence below contains an underlined word or phrase from the article. Following the sentence are three definitions. One definition is closest to the meaning of the underlined word. One definition is opposite or nearly opposite. Label those two definitions using the following key; do not label the remaining definition.

C—Closest   O—Opposite or Nearly Opposite

1. Why else would anyone have built such an <u>elaborate</u> pit?

_____ a. strange

_____ b. simple

_____ c. complicated

2. Once more they <u>resumed</u> digging.

_____ a. stopped

_____ b. continued

_____ c. tried

3. The next day the men returned, <u>brimming with</u> hope.

_____ a. full of

_____ b. looking for

_____ c. without

4. No amount of <u>bailing</u> with buckets or pumping could empty the pit.

_____ a. splashing

_____ b. removing

_____ c. filling

5. They had to <u>scramble</u> to escape with their lives.

_____ a. climb

_____ b. move slowly

_____ c. hurry

_____ Score 3 points for each correct C answer.

_____ Score 2 points for each correct O answer.

_____ **Total Score:** Using Words Precisely

Enter the four total scores in the spaces below, and add them together to find your Reading Comprehension Score. Then record your Reading Comprehension Score on the graph on page 57.

Score	Question Type	Lesson 2
_____	Finding the Main Idea	
_____	Recalling Facts	
_____	Making Inferences	
_____	Using Words Precisely	
_____	**Reading Comprehension Score**	

Author's Approach

Put an X in the box next to the correct answer.

1. The authors use the first sentence of the article to
   - ☐ a. entertain the reader.
   - ☐ b. establish the setting of the story.
   - ☐ c. describe Oak Island.

2. What is the authors' purpose in writing "The Money Pit"?
   - ☐ a. to describe the Money Pit and the attempts to reach the bottom
   - ☐ b. to persuade the reader to search for treasure in the Money Pit
   - ☐ c. to express an opinion about the Money Pit

3. The authors tell this story mainly by
   - ☐ a. comparing similar topics.
   - ☐ b. using their imagination and creativity.
   - ☐ c. giving details about the topic.

_____ Number of correct answers

Record your personal assessment of your work on the Critical Thinking Chart on page 58.

Summarizing and Paraphrasing

Follow the directions provided for question 1. Put an X in the box next to the correct answers for questions 2 and 3.

1. Look for the important ideas and events in paragraphs 12 and 13. Summarize those paragraphs in one or two sentences.

_____

_____

_____

_____

2. Complete the following one-sentence summary of the article using the lettered phrases from the phrase bank below. Write the letters on the lines.

```
Phrase bank:
a. an explanation of how Dan McGinnis found it
b. the various attempts that have been made to reach
   the bottom
c. speculation about who built the pit
```

The article about the Money Pit begins with _____, goes

on to explain _____, and ends with _____.

3. Choose the sentence that correctly restates the following sentence from the article: "There have been human costs as well."

☐ a. People have also spent a lot of money.

☐ b. Slaves were used too.

☐ c. People have lost their lives too.

```
_____ Number of correct answers

Record your personal assessment of your work on the
Critical Thinking Chart on page 58.
```

Critical Thinking

Follow the directions provided for questions 1, 4, and 5. Put an X in the box next to the correct answer for questions 2 and 3.

1. For each statement below, write O if it expresses an opinion or F if it expresses a fact.

_____ a. They were sure something big was buried there.

_____ b. Whoever built the pit had to be an engineer with a team of skilled miners.

_____ c. In 1804, they joined a company formed solely to find the treasure.

2. Based on the events in the article, you can predict that people will

☐ a. continue trying to reach the bottom of the Money Pit.

☐ b. discover that there is nothing in the Money Pit.

☐ c. stop digging in the Money Pit.

3. What was the effect of digging more than 90 feet into the Money Pit?

☐ a. A tunnel was created that led to the ocean.

☐ b. The pit filled with 60 feet of water.

☐ c. The workers reached the bottom of the pit.

4. There were attempts made to reach the bottom of the Money Pit in 1804 and 1849. List three ways in which these attempts and their outcomes were similar and three ways in which they were different.

Similarities

_____

_____

_____

Differences

_____

_____

_____

5. Which paragraphs provide evidence from the article that supports your answer to question 4?

_____

_____

_____ Number of correct answers

Record your personal assessment of your work on the Critical Thinking Chart on page 58.

Personal Response

I know the feeling

_____

_____

_____

Self-Assessment

One good question about this article that was not asked is

_____

_____

_____

The Man-Eaters of Tsavo

¹These days they're harmless. In fact, you can find them mounted and on display at Chicago's Field Museum. But when they were alive, they were a terror. There were only two of them, but they killed at will. People lost sleep worrying about who would be the next victim. One person died of shock just thinking about "the man-eaters of Tsavo."

2   In 1898 the British were building a railroad across east Africa. It was not an easy task. The tracks crossed mile

Today the lions that plagued the Tsavo area are mounted and on exhibit at Chicago's Field Museum. They killed more than 120 people while they were alive.

after mile of barren land. Food, water, and supplies had to be hauled in from far away. Skilled workers had to be brought in from the East Indies. Then, when the railroad workers reached the Tsavo River, they faced an even bigger problem. This new problem was lions—two huge lions that fed on human flesh.

3   Colonel John Henry Patterson was in charge of the railroad project. At first he didn't believe the workers' stories of lion attacks. He thought they were just rumors. Then one night he became convinced of the lions' existence. One of the lions snuck into the tent of a railroad worker. The lion grabbed the worker by the throat. As another worker watched in horror, he was dragged out of the tent. "Let go!" he cried. But the lion's grip was too strong. The next day, Patterson found the worker's remains. It was not a pretty sight.

4   The other workers, of course, were terrified. Many ran away or refused to work. Patterson was scared too. He also knew that the lions had to be killed. Otherwise, the railroad line would never get finished. Being a

skilled hunter, he decided that he would kill them himself. He didn't think it would be that hard to do. He was wrong.

5   That night Patterson, taking his rifle, climbed up into a tree near the area where the worker had been killed. There he waited for the lions. He had tied a goat to the tree, hoping this tasty meal would entice them. The lions, however, had a different meal in mind. Late that night, one of the cats attacked another tent, far away from the spot where Patterson was waiting, and dragged away another worker.

6   Patterson heard the victim's screams, but there was little he could do. Work camps stretched for eight miles along the railroad. He couldn't guard them all. Instead, he decided to build thick thorn fences around each camp. He thought that would keep the man-eaters out. The workers felt much safer with the fences in place. They also began keeping a fire burning in each camp throughout the night.

7   None of these safety measures worked, however. The lions never missed a meal. They either jumped over the fences or they crawled

through weak spots in them. Once again, the killings terrorized the workers.

8   Patterson was frightened, too. "In the whole of my life," he said, "I have never experienced anything more nerve shaking than to hear the deep roars of these dreadful monsters." When the roaring came closer, "[I knew] that some one or other of us was doomed to be their victim." Just before the lions entered a camp, their roaring ceased. That's when the men knew one of the lions was stalking its prey. Soon the beast would attack. But where? Patterson never seemed to guess right. He kept setting traps, but the lions kept striking someplace else. The lions, he later said, always seemed to know where his traps were.

9   At last, Patterson decided to try a new tactic. He would no longer wait for the lions to come to him. He would hunt the lions on their own ground. Day after day he crawled through the bushes. He never found them. That was probably just as well. If he had come across them, they would almost certainly have killed him before he could kill them.

10   Meanwhile, work on the railroad had come to a complete stop. Hundreds of workers had run away. Those who stayed could think of only one thing—how to stay safe. Some tied their beds up in trees. Others slept on the top of water tanks or roofs. Still others stayed in their tents but dug pits in the middle of the dirt floor. They slept in the pits, which they covered over with heavy logs.

11   One day Patterson came across a donkey that the lions had killed. They hadn't eaten all of it and Patterson thought they might return to finish their meal. So he built a platform near the donkey's body outside one of the camps. That night he sat on the top of the platform with his rifle and waited.

12   Soon one of the lions came near. With no moon, the night was black, and it was difficult to see. But Patterson could hear the lion's deep sigh. The animal was hungry. But it was not going after the donkey. It was going after Patterson! Slowly the lion circled the platform. Patterson sat there terrified, "hardly daring even to blink my eyes."

13   The lion came closer and closer. Still Patterson could not see it. Then at last he saw the lion's faint form crouched under a nearby bush. Patterson pulled the trigger of his rifle. The lion gave a terrific roar. It ran into the thick brush.

Patterson kept firing where he thought the lion was hiding. The lion's growls turned to moans. Then the night was silent. One of the man-eaters of Tsavo was dead.

14   The shooting woke up the whole camp. When the workers heard the news they gave a loud cheer. "Every man in camp came out," said Patterson, "tom toms split the night air and horns were blown as men came running to the scene." The workers danced the rest of the night away.

15   The dead lion was huge. It measured nearly nine feet in length and three and a half feet in height. (Male lions rarely grow more than eight feet in length and three feet in height.) It took eight men to carry its body to camp.

16   One lion was dead, but there was still one roaming free. For the second lion, Patterson used dead goats as bait. When the lion approached, he shot it in the shoulder. This lion, however, managed to slip away before he could shoot it again. Ten days later, the beast came back to get one of the men sleeping in a tree. This time Patterson was in the right place. He fired shots at the lion, but didn't kill it. The next night, Patterson climbed the same tree. When the lion returned, he shot it in the chest. Once again, the lion got away, badly wounded but not dead.

17   In the morning Patterson went after the lion. He knew it was injured, so he thought it would be easy to hunt it down. He spotted the lion hiding in some bushes. He fired his rifle. He hit the lion, but that didn't stop it from charging. Patterson shot it again and again. Each time the lion tumbled to the ground only to get up and charge once more. Finally, its leg shattered, the lion could barely move. Patterson killed it with another volley of shots. The lions' reign of terror was over. The workers returned to their jobs. By then, however, "the man-eaters of Tsavo" had claimed more than 120 lives.

If you have been timed while reading this article, enter your reading time below. Then turn to the Words-per-Minute Table on page 55 and look up your reading speed (words per minute). Enter your reading speed on the graph on page 56.

Reading Time: Lesson 3

———— : ————

Minutes   Seconds

A Finding the Main Idea

One statement below expresses the main idea of the article. One statement is too general, or too broad. The other statement explains only part of the article; it is too narrow. Label the statements using the following key:

M—Main Idea   **B—Too Broad**   **N—Too Narrow**

_____ 1. Two man-eating lions managed to halt work on a railroad in Africa and kill more than 120 people before being killed by Colonel Patterson.

_____ 2. Colonel Patterson had to fire several shots at the lions in order to kill them.

_____ 3. Man-eating lions terrorized people in the Tsavo area in Africa in the late 19th century.

_____ Score 15 points for a correct M answer.

_____ Score 5 points for each correct B or N answer.

_____ **Total Score:** Finding the Main Idea

B Recalling Facts

How well do you remember the facts in the article? Put an X in the box next to the answer that correctly completes each statement about the article.

1. Colonel Patterson became convinced of the existence of the lions when
   □ a. he heard the workers' stories.
   □ b. he found the remains of one of the workers.
   □ c. a lion grabbed him by the throat.

2. In order to protect the workers, Patterson decided to
   □ a. build thorn fences around each camp.
   □ b. feed goats to the lions.
   □ c. build pits in the workers' tents.

3. The workers knew a lion was about to attack when
   □ a. they heard its roar.
   □ b. they saw the beast.
   □ c. it grew silent.

4. Patterson drew one of the lions to the tree where he was hiding by
   □ a. tying his bed in the tree.
   □ b. building a platform.
   □ c. waiting near a donkey it had half-eaten.

5. In order to kill the second lion, Patterson had to
   □ a. shoot it several times over several days.
   □ b. tie a goat to a tree.
   □ c. build a platform.

Score 5 points for each correct answer.

_____ **Total Score:** Recalling Facts

C Making Inferences

When you combine your own experience with information from a text to draw a conclusion that is not directly stated in that text, you are making an inference. Below are five statements that may or may not be inferences based on information in the article. Label the statements using the following key:

C—Correct Inference   F—Faulty Inference

_____ 1. The lions liked the taste of human flesh more than the flesh of other animals.

_____ 2. Patterson volunteered to kill the lions because he knew he could outsmart them.

_____ 3. The railroad workers didn't have guns to protect themselves from the lions.

_____ 4. Lions cannot climb trees.

_____ 5. The lions of Tsavo were very strong.

Score 5 points for each correct answer.

_____ **Total Score:** Making Inferences

D Using Words Precisely

Each numbered sentence below contains an underlined word or phrase from the article. Following the sentence are three definitions. One definition is closest to the meaning of the underlined word. One definition is opposite or nearly opposite. Label those two definitions using the following key; do not label the remaining definition.

C—Closest   O—Opposite or Nearly Opposite

1. As another worker watched in horror, he was <u>dragged</u> out of the tent.

_____ a. thrown

_____ b. pulled

_____ c. pushed

2. He had tied a goat to the tree, hoping this tasty meal would <u>entice</u> them.

_____ a. attract

_____ b. bait

_____ c. disgust

3. Just before the lions entered a camp, their roaring <u>ceased</u>.

_____ a. stopped

_____ b. began

_____ c. became quieter

4. Then at last he saw the lion's faint form <u>crouched</u> under a nearby bush.

_____ a. sleeping

_____ b. lying close to the ground

_____ c. standing

5. Finally, its leg <u>shattered</u>, the lion could barely move.

_____ a. whole

_____ b. weak

_____ c. broken

_____ Score 3 points for each correct C answer.

_____ Score 2 points for each correct O answer.

_____ **Total Score:** Using Words Precisely

Enter the four total scores in the spaces below, and add them together to find your Reading Comprehension Score. Then record your Reading Comprehension Score on the graph on page 57.

Score	Question Type	Lesson 3
_____	Finding the Main Idea	
_____	Recalling Facts	
_____	Making Inferences	
_____	Using Words Precisely	
_____	**Reading Comprehension Score**	

Author's Approach

Put an X in the box next to the correct answer.

1. The authors use the first sentence of the article to

☐ a. get the reader's attention.

☐ b. inform the reader about the lions of Tsavo.

☐ c. describe the lions of Tsavo.

2. The main purpose of the second paragraph is to

☐ a. summarize the article.

☐ b. describe the setting of the article.

☐ c. introduce the characters in the article.

3. Which of the following statements from the article best describes Colonel Patterson's reasons for trying to kill the lions?

☐ a. Patterson was scared, too.

☐ b. At first he didn't believe the workers' stories of lion attacks.

☐ c. The railroad line would never get finished.

_____ Number of correct answers

Record your personal assessment of your work on the Critical Thinking Chart on page 58.

Summarizing and Paraphrasing

Follow the directions provided for questions 1 and 2. Put an X in the box next to the correct answer for question 3.

1. Reread paragraph 8 in the article. Below, write a summary of the paragraph in no more than 25 words.

_____

_____

_____

_____

Reread your summary and decide whether it covers the important ideas in the paragraph. Next, decide how to shorten the summary to 15 words or less without leaving out any essential information. Write this summary below.

_____

_____

_____

2. Look for the important ideas and events in paragraphs 11, 12, and 13. Summarize those paragraphs in one or two sentences.

_____

_____

_____

3. Choose the best one-sentence paraphrase for the following sentence from the article: "The lions' reign of terror was over."

☐ a. The lions were not a threat any longer.

☐ b. The workers were no longer frightened of the lions.

☐ c. There were no more lions in the Tsavo area.

_____ Number of correct answers

Record your personal assessment of your work on the Critical Thinking Chart on page 58.

Critical Thinking

Follow the directions provided for questions 1, 4, and 5. Put an X in the box next to the correct answer for questions 2 and 3.

1. For each statement below, write O if it expresses an opinion or F if it expresses a fact.

_____ a. He didn't think it would be that hard to do.

_____ b. Work camps stretched for eight miles along the railroad.

_____ c. The dead lion was huge.

2. From the article, you can conclude that if Colonel Patterson had not killed the lions,

☐ a. someone else would have killed them.

☐ b. the lions would have stopped terrorizing the railroad workers.

☐ c. the railroad would not have been completed.

3. What was the effect of Patterson waiting for the lions near a half-eaten donkey?

☐ a. Another person in the camp was killed.

☐ b. Patterson was able to kill one of the lions.

☐ c. Patterson built a platform near the donkey.

4. In which paragraph did you find the information you needed to answer question 3?

_____

5. Choose from the letters in the phrase bank below to correctly complete the following statement. Write the letters on the lines.

Phrase bank:
a. the railroad workers
b. work on the railroad stopped
c. fear for their lives

According to the article, two man-eating lions caused

_____ to _____, and the effect was _____.

_____ Number of correct answers

Record your personal assessment of your work on the Critical Thinking Chart on page 58.

Personal Response

I know how Colonel Patterson felt when he was hunting the lions because

_____

_____

_____

_____

Self-Assessment

A word or phrase in the article that I do not understand is

_____

_____

_____

_____

The Evil Eye

[1]Bad luck seemed to follow Spain's King Alfonso. In 1923, he sailed to Italy. Some Italians rowed out to greet him. As they approached the king, a wave hit their boat. Several men were washed overboard and drowned. The Italians tried to continue with their welcome. One boat fired a cannon in Alfonso's honor. The cannon blew up, killing the crew. Next a naval officer shook the king's hand. A short time later the officer dropped dead.

2   Finally, the Italians took the king on a tour around a local lake. But

In many countries the image of an eye is often painted on the front of a boat. Some people believe that this keeps the boat safe from the curse of the evil eye.

during the tour the lake's dam burst. Fifty people drowned. Hundreds of others saw their homes washed away before their eyes.

3   Was it just coincidence? Benito Mussolini, the leader of Italy at that time, didn't think so. He refused to meet with Alfonso. Instead, he sent an advisor to meet with him. Mussolini stayed away from Alfonso because he was sure the king had *the evil eye.* Mussolini did not want that deadly eye turned on him.

4   Belief in the evil eye is very old. It is often brought up when things go wrong. People have blamed the evil eye for crop failures. They have used it to explain the sickness of animals. They have even said the evil eye causes death. One ancient Jewish book issued this dire warning: "For every [person] that dies of natural causes, ninety-nine will die of the evil eye."

5   What exactly is the evil eye? Believers say it is a powerful look that can be given at any time. The one who gives it might be trying to curse you. On the other hand, he or she might not be aware of what is happening. Either way, they say, the person has a dark and dangerous force dwelling in his or her soul. When that force is trained on you, trouble is sure to come your way.

6   Who has the evil eye, according to believers? There are many answers to that question. Often people who look a bit different are thought to have it. In Turkey, that means people with blue eyes. In parts of Africa it means those with squinty eyes. In other places it means someone who is cross-eyed or left-handed or childless.

7   In the past true believers went to great lengths to protect themselves from the evil eye. The color red was thought to protect against it, so Italian brides often covered their heads with red veils. In Scotland farmers tied red ribbons to the tails of their livestock. In the 17th century even judges were afraid. Some judges made defendants enter the court *backwards!* That way the defendants couldn't look them in the eye.

8   Today some people still believe in the evil eye and work hard to avoid it.

They wear special charms to keep themselves safe. These charms may be in the shape of an eye or a hand or a horseshoe. In Greece and Turkey a blue glass eye charm is used. This eye supposedly acts as a mirror. If the evil eye is thrown at the wearer, the glass eye will bounce the evil back in the other direction.

9   Fishing boats in Europe often have an eye painted on the bow to ward off the evil eye. Garlic and sage are used in some places. In the United States and Canada farmers often nail a horseshoe over their barn doors. In the Middle East some people carry two marbles with them at all times. One is black and one is white. The white marble protects them in the daytime. The black marble protects them at night.

10   Those who believe in the evil eye say that it is most dangerous to babies. So some parents keep their newborn in the house for the first month. Sooner or later, though, they have to take the child out into the world. Here the danger is great. Many people want to look at the baby, but one of them might have the evil eye. Parents live in fear that a stranger will praise their child. They dread hearing the words, "Oh, what a pretty baby!" They believe that praise can be a curse sent by someone with the evil eye.

11   Friends of the parents know how to compliment the baby safely. They rub a bit of dirt on the child's clothes. Then they say, "What a pretty baby— too bad she is so dirty." Because they have found something bad to say, the parents know that no curse is being sent.

12   If the evil eye is given to the baby, parents must act quickly. They must spit on their child. Or they must say something bad about the child to cancel out the curse.

13   There are other ways to break the evil eye curse. One way is to have someone pass a raw egg over the cursed person's face and then break the egg. You could try piercing a lemon with nails. If that doesn't work, you should spit at the person with the evil eye three times.

14   How can you be sure that *you* don't have the evil eye? You can't. Most of you are probably okay. But just in case, be sure not to stare at people. It isn't polite, and besides, you might wind up with a bunch of people spitting back at you!

If you have been timed while reading this article, enter your reading time below. Then turn to the Words-per-Minute Table on page 55 and look up your reading speed (words per minute). Enter your reading speed on the graph on page 56.

Reading Time: Lesson 4

——————— : ———————
Minutes   Seconds

A | Finding the Main Idea

One statement below expresses the main idea of the article. One statement is too general, or too broad. The other statement explains only part of the article; it is too narrow. Label the statements using the following key:

M—Main Idea **B—Too Broad** **N—Too Narrow**

_____ 1. For centuries, people have tried to protect themselves from the evil eye, which they believe can cause crop failures, sickness, and even death.

_____ 2. Benito Mussolini believed King Alfonso of Spain had the evil eye.

_____ 3. Belief in the evil eye is very old.

_____ Score 15 points for a correct M answer.

_____ Score 5 points for each correct B or N answer.

_____ **Total Score:** Finding the Main Idea

B | Recalling Facts

How well do you remember the facts in the article? Put an X in the box next to the answer that correctly completes each statement about the article.

1. The evil eye is a
☐ a. terrible illness.
☐ b. curse.
☐ c. powerful look that can be given at any time.

2. Who is thought to have the evil eye?
☐ a. left-handed people
☐ b. babies
☐ c. people with brown eyes

3. You can protect yourself from the evil eye by wearing
☐ a. blue.
☐ b. a glass eye charm.
☐ c. glasses.

4. The group of people most easily harmed by the evil eye is
☐ a. farmers.
☐ b. Italians.
☐ c. babies.

5. According to the story, which of these will *not* break the evil eye curse?
☐ a. spitting at the person who has the evil eye
☐ b. washing in sea water
☐ c. saying something bad about the person who was cursed

Score 5 points for each correct answer.

_____ **Total Score:** Recalling Facts

C Making Inferences

When you combine your own experience with information from a text to draw a conclusion that is not directly stated in that text, you are making an inference. Below are five statements that may or may not be inferences based on information in the article. Label the statements using the following key:

C—Correct Inference   F—Faulty Inference

_____ 1. In Turkey, there are not many people with blue eyes.

_____ 2. Italian brides were afraid of being cursed by the evil eye.

_____ 3. Only people with the evil eye give compliments.

_____ 4. People all around the world believe in the evil eye.

_____ 5. King Alfonso of Spain didn't like Benito Mussolini.

Score 5 points for each correct answer.

_____ **Total Score:** Making Inferences

D Using Words Precisely

Each numbered sentence below contains an underlined word or phrase from the article. Following the sentence are three definitions. One definition is closest to the meaning of the underlined word. One definition is opposite or nearly opposite. Label those two definitions using the following key. Do not label the remaining definition.

C—Closest   O—Opposite or Nearly Opposite

1. But during the tour, the lake's dam <u>burst</u>.

_____ a. broke

_____ b. cracked

_____ c. held together

2. Either way, the person has a dark and dangerous force <u>dwelling in</u> his or her soul.

_____ a. taking over

_____ b. far from

_____ c. living in

3. In parts of Africa it means those with <u>squinty</u> eyes.

_____ a. slanted

_____ b. half-closed

_____ c. large, open

4. They <u>dread</u> hearing the words, "Oh, what a pretty baby."

_____ a. fear

_____ b. dislike

_____ c. look forward to

5. In Scotland, farmers tied red ribbons to the tails of their <u>livestock</u>.

_____ a. crops

_____ b. farm animals

_____ c. pets

_____ Score 3 points for each correct C answer.

_____ Score 2 points for each correct O answer.

_____ **Total Score:** Using Words Precisely

Enter the four total scores in the spaces below, and add them together to find your Reading Comprehension Score. Then record your Reading Comprehension Score on the graph on page 57.

Score	Question Type	Lesson 4
_____	Finding the Main Idea	
_____	Recalling Facts	
_____	Making Inferences	
_____	Using Words Precisely	
_____	**Reading Comprehension Score**	

Author's Approach

Put an X in the box next to the correct answer.

1. The authors use the first sentence of the article to

☐ a. inform the reader about the evil eye.

☐ b. get the reader's attention.

☐ c. describe King Alfonso.

2. The authors probably wrote this article in order to

☐ a. inform and entertain the reader.

☐ b. scare the reader.

☐ c. make fun of people who believe in the evil eye.

3. After reading "The Evil Eye," you can conclude that the authors

☐ a. believe in the evil eye.

☐ b. do not believe in the evil eye.

☐ c. do not give their opinion about the evil eye.

_____ Number of correct answers

Record your personal assessment of your work on the Critical Thinking Chart on page 58.

Summarizing and Paraphrasing

Follow the directions provided for question 1. Put an X in the box next to the correct answer for the other questions.

1. Look for the important ideas and events in paragraphs 5 and 6. Summarize those paragraphs in one or two sentences.

_____

_____

_____

_____

2. Read the statement from the article below. Then read the paraphrase of that statement. Choose the reason that best tells why the paraphrase does not say the same thing as the statement.

   Statement: "Often people who look a bit different are thought to have [the evil eye]."

   Paraphrase: Some people believe that blue-eyed people have the evil eye.

   ☐ a. Paraphrase says too much.

   ☐ b. Paraphrase doesn't say enough.

   ☐ c. Paraphrase doesn't agree with the statement about the article.

3. Choose the best one-sentence paraphrase for the following sentence from the article: "Friends of the parents know how to compliment the baby safely."

   ☐ a. Friends of the parents don't have the evil eye.

   ☐ b. The parents' friends know how to give a compliment without cursing the baby.

   ☐ c. There are certain ways of complimenting a baby that are safe.

_____ Number of correct answers

Record your personal assessment of your work on the Critical Thinking Chart on page 58.

Critical Thinking

Put an X in the box next to the correct answer.

1. According to the article, what is the effect of wearing a glass eye charm?

   ☐ a. to give someone the evil eye

   ☐ b. to break the evil eye curse

   ☐ c. to protect the wearer from the evil eye

2. From what the article told you about the evil eye, you can conclude that

   ☐ a. some people still believe in the evil eye.

   ☐ b. brides in Italy still wear red veils.

   ☐ c. many people have died because of the evil eye.

3. What did you have to do to answer question 2?

☐ a. find an opinion (what someone thinks about something)

☐ b. draw a conclusion (a sensible statement based on the text and your experience)

☐ c. find a reason (why something is the way it is)

4. Which of the following statements from the article is an opinion rather than a fact?

☐ a. Bad luck seemed to follow Spain's King Alfonso.

☐ b. Belief in the evil eye is very old.

☐ c. Fishing boats in Europe often have an eye painted on the bow to ward off the evil eye.

5. What is the effect of the evil eye, according to those who believe in it?

☐ a. They try to protect themselves from it.

☐ b. A dark and dangerous force dwells in some people's souls.

☐ c. It can cause sickness and death.

_____ Number of correct answers

Record your personal assessment of your work on the Critical Thinking Chart on page 58.

Personal Response

I wonder why

_____

_____

_____

_____

Self-Assessment

From reading this article, I have learned

_____

_____

_____

_____

The Rainmaker

[1]San Diego needed rain. Even in a good year, only about 10 inches of rain fall on this California city. But in the late 1800s, that number was way down. Severe droughts were hurting the city. If San Diego wanted to grow in size and wealth, it needed water.

2   In 1897 the city came up with a plan. It built Morena Dam on a nearby river. The dam created a lake, or reservoir, to store rainwater. The dam seemed like a good solution. But it didn't work. There was never enough rain to fill up the reservoir.

Charles Hatfield claimed that the 23 chemicals he mixed together could "make" rain. Here he is mixing the "rain stew" that brought a record 38 inches of rain to the city of San Diego.

3   By 1915 it was clear that something else had to be done. But what?

4   Enter Charles Hatfield, the rainmaker. He said he could make it rain. Only a few people believed him. Most thought he was a fraud. Still, he did seem to have a knack for bringing rain. At least, it seemed to rain when and where he said it would.

5   Eleven years earlier, Hatfield had been in Los Angeles, California, another dry city. Merchants there had promised Hatfield $50 if he could produce one inch of rain. Hatfield agreed. He told the merchants they would get their inch of rain within five days. And indeed, on the fourth day more than an inch of rain fell on Los Angeles. Hatfield walked away with $50.

6   Soon after that, a Los Angeles newspaper got in touch with Hatfield. It asked him to make 18 inches of rain fall in the first five months of 1905. If he did, the paper would pay him $1,000. Everyone thought it was a gag. They assumed it was just a way to sell papers. After all, it almost never rains that much in Los Angeles.

Still, by the end of May, 18.22 inches of rain had fallen!

7   Hatfield claimed he brought the rain with a special "rain stew." First, he built a 20-foot-tall tower. Then he mixed up a batch of 23 different chemicals. He never revealed the formula. He did not even tell Paul, his brother and partner. Hatfield mixed all the chemicals together over a fire at the top of the tower and let the mixture evaporate into the air.

8   When people in San Diego heard about Hatfield, some wanted to hire him. A group called the Wide Awake Improvement Club thought it was worth a try. But the city council said no. Its members still hoped the dam was all they needed. The debate went on for years. So, too, did the dry weather.

9   Then in December 1915, Hatfield showed up at Morena Dam. He boasted that he could fill the reservoir. He said he could make it rain at least 40 inches within a year. The city would then have all the water it needed. His fee for this feat, he said, was $10,000. By this time the city

council was desperate. The members felt they had nothing to lose. So they agreed to hire him. The council members, however, did not sign the contract. But Hatfield did not notice. Or maybe he just thought their word was good enough.

10   In any case, on January 13, 1916, Hatfield and his brother Paul put up a 20-foot tower near Morena Dam. They laid a platform on the top and built a fire on it. Hatfield mixed his "rain stew" in a pot over the fire. Then he released the steam into the air and waited.

11   He did not have to wait long. The next morning clouds began to roll in. By noon it was raining hard. Still Hatfield kept his pot boiling. The Wide Awake Improvement Club was thrilled. So, too, was everyone else. Suddenly the city's future looked bright. One newspaper headline proclaimed: "Downpour Lays Mantle of Wealth on San Diego."

12   For the next four days the rain came down in buckets. By the third day, people were starting to worry. They had never seen this much rain

before. The whole month of January usually brought less than two inches of rain. Now close to 13 inches had fallen in just four days. Roads were under water. Floods washed out bridges. Homes floated away. Railroad tracks became swamped. People on one train had to be carried to dry land by boat! One man joked that the city should pay Hatfield $100,000 to *stop* the rain.

13 At last, on January 20, the rain stopped. The sun came out. It looked as if the worst was over. But it wasn't. Six days later the rain started again, harder than ever. The ground could not absorb any more water. The San Diego River overflowed its banks. More homes got washed away. All but two of the city's 112 bridges were swept away. At the Morena Dam the water level rose two feet an hour. Frightened engineers had to divert water away from the dam. Still the water level came within five inches of the top. Luckily, it didn't overflow. If it had, the resulting flood could have wiped out the whole city.

14 On January 29 the rain finally did end. By then 38 inches had fallen on San Diego. That was a record that still stands.

15 That day Charles and Paul Hatfield took down their tower. They swept up all clues as to the chemicals they had used. But as they worked, they heard that a lynch mob was headed their way. An angry throng of citizens vowed to kill Hatfield for flooding their city. The brothers slipped out of town before the mob could catch them.

16 Later, Hatfield tried to explain that the damage was not his fault. He said the city council was to blame. He had only done what they asked him to do. Maybe, he said, they shouldn't have wanted so much rain.

17 Hatfield tried to collect the $10,000 the city owed him. The council flatly refused to pay. The members pointed out that they had never signed the contract. They also pointed out the damage that had been done to the city by the rain. Hatfield then lowered his demand to $4,000. That, he said, would just cover the cost of his chemicals. Still the council said no. In the end Hatfield got nothing from the city.

18 Did Charles Hatfield really cause the rain? Some people say he did. They think his foul-smelling "rain stew" did work. Years later, his brother Paul said, "After all, they are beginning to seed clouds [with chemicals] to make rain." Others disagree. They believe Hatfield was just lucky and a very good student of weather trends. They think he studied weather records and rain cycles and then guessed right about when it was going to rain. To this day no one knows the truth. So Hatfield the Rainmaker remains one of the mysteries of history.

If you have been timed while reading this article, enter your reading time below. Then turn to the Words-per-Minute Table on page 55 and look up your reading speed (words per minute). Enter your reading speed on the graph on page 56.

Reading Time: Lesson 5

_____ : _____
Minutes   Seconds

A Finding the Main Idea

One statement below expresses the main idea of the article. One statement is too general, or too broad. The other statement explains only part of the article; it is too narrow. Label the statements using the following key:

M—Main Idea   **B—Too Broad**   **N—Too Narrow**

_____ 1. Although many people didn't believe Charles Hatfield could make rain, it often did rain when he released his "rain stew" into the air.

_____ 2. In the early 1900s "rainmakers" traveled to dry cities claiming they could create rain.

_____ 3. In 1916 Charles Hatfield may have been responsible for the 38 inches of rain that flooded San Diego.

_____ Score 15 points for a correct M answer.

_____ Score 5 points for each correct B or N answer.

_____ **Total Score:** Finding the Main Idea

B Recalling Facts

How well do you remember the facts in the article? Put an X in the box next to the answer that correctly completes each statement about the article.

1. City officials built Morena Dam near San Diego to
☐ a. make rain.
☐ b. store rainwater.
☐ c. bring money to the city.

2. In 1904 the merchants in Los Angeles offered to pay Charles Hatfield $50 if he could
☐ a. bring rain to the city within five days.
☐ b. produce 18 inches of rain.
☐ c. produce one inch of rain.

3. Hatfield created his "rain stew" by
☐ a. mixing together 23 different chemicals.
☐ b. building a 20-foot-tall tower.
☐ c. releasing water vapor into the air.

4. Four days after the Hatfields set up their rain tower in San Diego,
☐ a. the city paid them $100,000 to stop the rain.
☐ b. 38 inches of rain had already fallen.
☐ c. roads were underwater and houses had been swept away.

5. By the time the rain ended,
☐ a. 110 bridges had been washed away.
☐ b. the whole city had been wiped out.
☐ c. Morena Dam had overflowed.

Score 5 points for each correct answer.

_____ **Total Score:** Recalling Facts

C Making Inferences

When you combine your own experience with information from a text to draw a conclusion that is not directly stated in that text, you are making an inference. Below are five statements that may or may not be inferences based on information in the article. Label the statements using the following key:

C—Correct Inference   **F—Faulty Inference**

_____ 1. The chemicals Charles Hatfield mixed together created rain.

_____ 2. The city of San Diego did not hire Charles Hatfield a second time.

_____ 3. The Hatfields became rich by "making rain."

_____ 4. Cities on the West Coast often have problems getting enough water.

_____ 5. Some people in San Diego believed that Hatfield had brought the rain.

Score 5 points for each correct answer.

_____ **Total Score:** Making Inferences

D Using Words Precisely

Each numbered sentence below contains an underlined word or phrase from the article. Following the sentence are three definitions. One definition is closest to the meaning of the underlined word. One definition is opposite or nearly opposite. Label those two definitions using the following key; do not label the remaining definition.

C—Closest   O—Opposite or Nearly Opposite

1. Most thought he was a fraud.

_____ a. believable

_____ b. genuine

_____ c. a fake

2. Still, he seemed to have a knack for bringing rain.

_____ a. talent

_____ b. method

_____ c. lack of ability

3. He boasted that he could fill the reservoir.

_____ a. said with pride

_____ b. shouted

_____ c. wasn't sure

4. Suddenly the city's future looked bright.

_____ a. uncertain

_____ b. promising

_____ c. sunny

5. The brothers <u>slipped</u> out of town before the mob could catch them.

_____ a. went quietly

_____ b. went conspicuously

_____ c. fell

_____ Score 3 points for each correct C answer.

_____ Score 2 points for each correct O answer.

_____ **Total Score:** Using Words Precisely

Enter the four total scores in the spaces below, and add them together to find your Reading Comprehension Score. Then record your Reading Comprehension Score on the graph on page 57.

Score	Question Type	Lesson 5
_____	Finding the Main Idea	
_____	Recalling Facts	
_____	Making Inferences	
_____	Using Words Precisely	
_____	**Reading Comprehension Score**	

Author's Approach

Put an X in the box next to the correct answer.

1. What is the authors' opinion of Charles Hatfield?

☐ a. The authors do not believe that Charles Hatfield could make rain.

☐ b. The authors believe that Charles Hatfield could make rain.

☐ c. The authors do not express their opinion of Charles Hatfield.

2. What is the authors' main purpose in writing "The Rainmaker"?

☐ a. to describe Charles Hatfield and his work

☐ b. to entertain the reader

☐ c. to express an opinion about Charles Hatfield

3. Which of the following statements from the article best describes the general opinion about Charles Hatfield in his time?

☐ a. Only a few people believed him.

☐ b. They think his foul-smelling "rain stew" did work.

☐ c. When people in San Diego heard about Hatfield, some wanted to hire him.

_____ Number of correct answers

Record your personal assessment of your work on the Critical Thinking Chart on page 58.

Summarizing and Paraphrasing

Follow the directions provided for questions 1 and 2. Put an X in the box next to the correct answer for question 3.

1. Reread paragraph 11 in the article. Below, write a summary of the paragraph in no more than 25 words.

_____

_____

_____

Reread your summary and decide whether it covers the important ideas in the paragraph. Next, decide how to shorten the summary to 15 words or less without leaving out any essential information. Write this summary below.

_____

_____

_____

2. Look for the important ideas and events in paragraphs 15 and 16. Summarize those paragraphs in one or two sentences.

_____

_____

_____

3. Read the newspaper headline from the article below. Then read the paraphrase of that headline. Choose the reason that best tells why the paraphrase does not say the same thing as the headline.

   Statement: "Downpour Lays Mantle of Wealth on San Diego."

   Paraphrase: Large quantity of rain covers San Diego.

   ☐ a. Paraphrase says too much.

   ☐ b. Paraphrase doesn't say enough.

   ☐ c. Paraphrase doesn't agree with the statement.

   _____ Number of correct answers

   Record your personal assessment of your work on the Critical Thinking Chart on page 58.

Critical Thinking

Follow the directions provided for questions 1 and 2. Put an X in the box next to the correct answer for questions 3 and 4.

1. For each statement below, write O if it expresses an opinion or F if it expresses a fact.

   _____ a. He seemed to have a knack for bringing rain.

   _____ b. By the end of May, 18.22 inches of rain had fallen.

   _____ c. Suddenly the city's future looked bright.

2. Choose from the letters below to correctly complete the following statement. Write the letters on the lines.

According to paragraph 13, _____ because _____.

a. the water level in the Morena Dam rose two feet an hour

b. many houses were swept away

c. the San Diego river overflowed its banks

3. From the information in the article, you can predict that

☐ a. Charles Hatfield stopped making rain after 1916.

☐ b. most people believed that Charles Hatfield really could make rain after it rained nearly 40 inches in San Diego.

☐ c. the city of San Diego did not hire Charles Hatfield a second time.

4. What did you have to do to answer question 3?

☐ a. find a cause (why something happened)

☐ b. find a summary (synthesized information)

☐ c. draw a conclusion (a logical statement based on the text and your experience)

_____ Number of correct answers

Record your personal assessment of your work on the Critical Thinking Chart on page 58.

Personal Response

What was most surprising or interesting to you about this article?

_____

_____

_____

_____

Self-Assessment

I really can't understand how

_____

_____

_____

_____

Compare and Contrast

Think about the articles you have read in Unit One. Pick the three articles you thought were the hardest to explain. Write the titles of the articles in the first column of the chart below. Use information you have learned from the articles to fill in the empty boxes in the chart.

Title	Was the mysterious event in this article explained in the end? If so, what was the explanation?	Which explanations presented in the article do you think are the most believable?	What explanations, besides those in the article, can you suggest for the occurrences in this article?

If you could choose one of these cases to investigate further, which one would it be? Why?

_____

_____

Words-per-Minute Table

Unit One

Directions: If you were timed while reading an article, refer to the Reading Time you recorded in the box at the end of the article. Use this Words-per-Minute Table to determine your reading speed for that article. Then plot your reading speed on the graph on page 56.

Minutes and Seconds

Lesson No. of Words	Sample 980	1 1011	2 1243	3 1231	4 887	5 1130	Seconds
1:30	653	674	829	821	591	753	**90**
1:40	588	607	746	739	532	678	**100**
1:50	535	551	678	671	484	616	**110**
2:00	490	506	622	616	444	565	**120**
2:10	452	467	574	568	409	522	**130**
2:20	420	433	533	528	380	484	**140**
2:30	392	404	497	492	355	452	**150**
2:40	368	379	466	462	333	424	**160**
2:50	346	357	439	434	313	399	**170**
3:00	327	337	414	410	296	377	**180**
3:10	309	319	393	389	280	357	**190**
3:20	294	303	373	369	266	339	**200**
3:30	280	289	355	352	253	323	**210**
3:40	267	276	339	336	242	308	**220**
3:50	256	264	324	321	231	295	**230**
4:00	245	253	311	308	222	283	**240**
4:10	235	243	298	295	213	271	**250**
4:20	226	233	287	284	205	261	**260**
4:30	218	225	276	274	197	251	**270**
4:40	210	217	266	264	190	242	**280**
4:50	203	209	257	255	184	234	**290**
5:00	196	202	249	246	177	226	**300**
5:10	190	196	241	238	172	219	**310**
5:20	184	190	233	231	166	212	**320**
5:30	178	184	226	224	161	205	**330**
5:40	173	178	219	217	157	199	**340**
5:50	168	173	213	211	152	194	**350**
6:00	163	169	207	205	148	188	**360**
6:10	159	164	202	200	144	183	**370**
6:20	155	160	196	194	140	178	**380**
6:30	151	156	191	189	136	174	**390**
6:40	147	152	186	185	133	170	**400**
6:50	143	148	182	180	130	165	**410**
7:00	140	144	178	176	127	161	**420**
7:10	137	141	173	172	124	158	**430**
7:20	134	138	170	168	121	154	**440**
7:30	131	135	166	164	118	151	**450**
7:40	128	132	162	161	116	147	**460**
7:50	125	129	159	157	113	144	**470**
8:00	123	126	155	154	111	141	**480**

Plotting Your Progress: Reading Speed

Unit One

Directions: If you were timed while reading an article, write your words-per-minute rate for that article in the box under the number of the lesson. Then plot your reading speed on the graph by putting a small X on the line directly above the number of the lesson, across from the number of words per minute you read. As you mark your speed for each lesson, graph your progress by drawing a line to connect the X's.

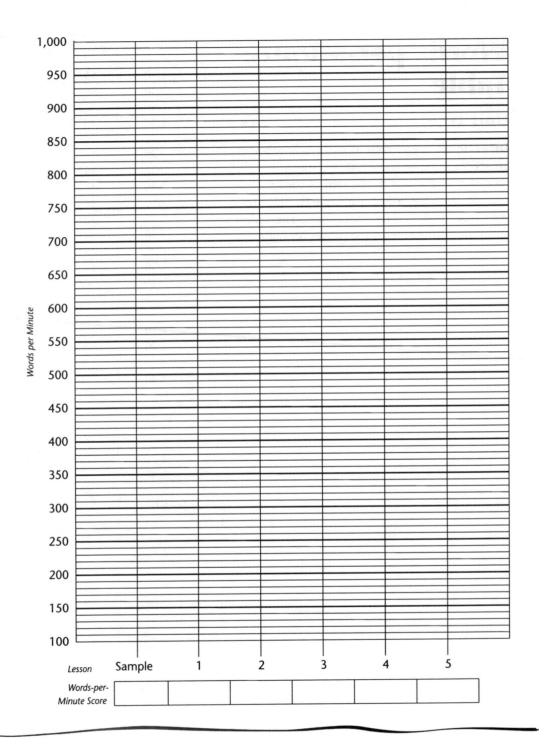

Plotting Your Progress: Reading Comprehension

Unit One

Directions: Write your Reading Comprehension score for each lesson in the box under the number of the lesson. Then plot your score on the graph by putting a small X on the line directly above the number of the lesson and across from the score you earned. As you mark your score for each lesson, graph your progress by drawing a line to connect the X's.

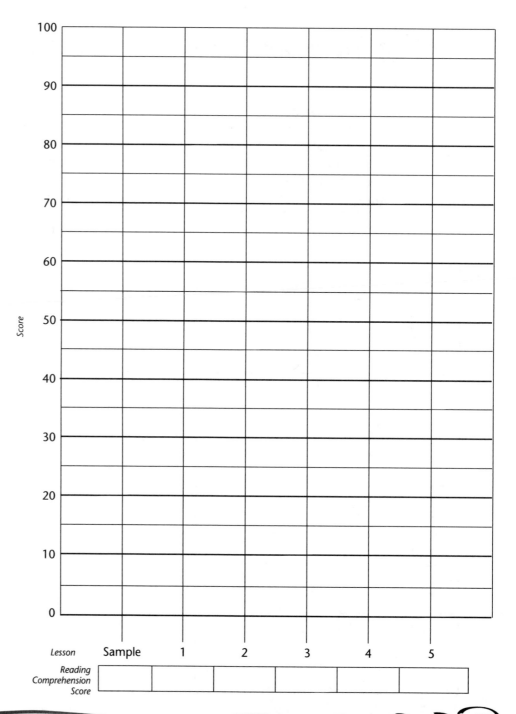

Plotting Your Progress: Critical Thinking

Unit One

Directions: Work with your teacher to evaluate your responses to the Critical Thinking questions for each lesson. Then fill in the appropriate spaces in the chart below. For each lesson and each type of Critical Thinking question, do the following: Mark a minus sign (−) in the box to indicate areas in which you feel you could improve. Mark a plus sign (+) to indicate areas in which you feel you did well. Mark a minus-slash-plus sign (−/+) to indicate areas in which you had mixed success. Then write any comments you have about your performance, including ideas for improvement.

Lesson	Author's Approach	Summarizing and Paraphrasing	Critical Thinking
Sample			
1			
2			
3			
4			
5			

UNIT TWO

What Happened to Amy?

MISSING PERSON

March 24, 1998

AMY BRADLEY

DESCRIPTION

Date of Birth: May 12, 1974
Sex: Female
Height: 5'6"
Weight: 120 pounds

Hair: Short Brown
Eyes: Green
Race: White

THE DETAILS

Amy Bradley was reported missing in the early morning hours of March 24, 1998. She was last seen by family members sitting on the balcony outside their cabin aboard the Rhapsody of the Seas cruise ship. The ship was en route to Curacao, Antilles at the time Amy was last seen. The ship docked in Curacao shortly after Amy was discovered missing. Extensive searches on the ship and at sea have produced no signs of Amy's whereabouts. This investigation is ongoing.

REMARKS

A reward is being offered for information leading to Amy Bradley's safe return.

Amy Bradley recently graduated from a college in Virginia with a degree in physical education. She enjoys playing basketball. She would have begun a job working with a computer company her return from the trip.

¹Amy Bradley seemed to have it all. The 23-year-old Virginian was smart, athletic, and beautiful. She had been a star basketball player in college. Now, in early 1998, she had just moved into a new apartment. She was about to start a new job. Best of all, she had been invited to go on a cruise with her parents and 21-year-old brother, Brad. But while on that cruise, something went wrong. Amy ended up missing. The story of how she vanished is both chilling and puzzling.

2   The first two days of the cruise went smoothly. Amy sent postcards to friends and picked up souvenirs to take home. She went swimming with

Because Amy Bradley has never been found, she remains on the FBI's Missing Persons list.

her dad and shopping with her mom. She and Brad checked out the ship's casino. As she moved around the ship, Amy was careful not to get near the railing. She was afraid of heights. She was also afraid of ocean water. Amy didn't worry about drowning—in fact, she was a certified lifeguard. But she was squeamish about ocean creatures. She didn't like the idea of being in the water with sharks and jellyfish.

3   Being attractive and outgoing, Amy received a lot of attention from the ship's passengers and crew. In those first two days she learned the names of several crew members. They all seemed friendly, and Amy had fun talking with them. One of these new acquaintances was a band member on the ship. Everyone called him "Yellow."

4   On the night of March 23, the third day of the trip, Brad and Amy went dancing in the ship's disco after enjoying a formal dinner with their parents. Yellow was there, and Amy talked with him for a while. She and Brad didn't return to their family's quarters until 3:45 the next morning. At that point Brad went to bed. Amy stretched out on a lounge chair on the balcony out-side the cabin. She was feeling a little seasick and wanted the fresh air.

5   At about 5:30 A.M., Amy's father woke up and glanced out onto the balcony. He could not see Amy's face, but he did see her legs and feet on the lounge chair. Figuring she had fallen asleep out there, he saw no reason to rouse her. Instead, he just went back to sleep.

6   Half an hour later he thought he heard someone leaving the cabin. Waking up, he saw that Amy was gone. That surprised him because normally she was a late sleeper. Mr. Bradley knew she usually left notes telling the family where she had gone. So he looked around for one. But there was no note. Perplexed, he decided to go up to the main deck to look for her. For almost an hour, Mr. Bradley searched for Amy. He found no trace of her anywhere.

7   With panic rising in his chest, Mr. Bradley found one of the ship's officers. He told the man Amy was missing. What happened next is in dispute. The Bradleys don't think the crew reacted with proper speed or concern. The cruise line, on the other hand, says the crew did everything they should have done. The ship's officers did not want to alarm the other guests. They thought Amy might be in someone's cabin or off in some little-used part of the ship.

8   By this time the ship had docked at the Caribbean island of Curacao. The Bradleys begged the officers to keep everyone on board until their daughter was found. But the officers didn't think that would be fair to the other passengers. So the gangplank was lowered, and many of the guests went ashore.

9   As the hours slipped by and there was still no sign of Amy, the Bradley family grew more and more frantic. Crew members, too, became more concerned. A search was made of the entire ship, but Amy wasn't found. Officials then began a search of the water. For three days planes and boats looked for Amy. The F.B.I. was called in. They found nothing.

10   What could have happened? At first the F.B.I. wondered if Amy had killed herself by jumping overboard. But that didn't make sense. Everyone agreed she was a happy young woman with many

plans for the future. She might have fallen overboard by accident. But that didn't seem likely, either. The railing came up to her chest. Besides, as her family said, it made her weak in the knees just to get near the ship's railing. Also, no body was found in the waters around Curacao.

11 Had Amy run away? She could have put on a disguise. Then she could have walked off the ship with the other passengers in Curacao. The F.B.I. considered this. But nothing about Amy fit the "runaway profile." She really had nothing to run away from. She got along very well with her family. She had plenty of friends and had recently adopted a dog. While on the trip, she had bought artwork for her new apartment and gifts for her friends.

12 That left the possibility of foul play. Could Amy have been kidnapped? Could a passenger or crew member have drugged her or cornered her somehow? Could the kidnapper have hidden her until he or she found a way to get her off the ship?

13 This idea terrified the Bradleys. But two clues seemed to point in that direction. First of all, two teenage girls on board the ship claimed to have seen Amy the morning she disappeared. They said she was with Yellow, the band member who had been so friendly.

According to them, Amy and Yellow had been headed up to the disco room around 5:30 A.M. About 15 minutes later Yellow had left that room alone.

14 The second clue came from a police trainee in Puerto Rico. He claimed he saw Amy on March 28. That was four days after she disappeared. It was also the day the ship stopped in Puerto Rico before heading back to the United States. The trainee said he saw a man forcing Amy into a taxi. He said she looked upset and confused. When the F.B.I. questioned the trainee, he was indeed able to pick Amy's picture out of a line-up.

15 These clues pointed to trouble. But they also left many questions unanswered. For one thing, why had Amy left the family cabin so early on the morning of March 24? Where had she been going? Why didn't she leave a note?

16 Also, what motive would anyone have had for kidnapping her? Amy wasn't rich. She had no enemies. And if someone had nabbed her, where had she been hidden? Had she been somewhere on the ship as it sailed from Curacao to Puerto Rico? If so, why wasn't she found when the ship was searched? And why was no ransom note ever sent?

17 Finally, there was the question of Yellow. Had Amy really gone up to the disco room with him on the morning

of March 24? If so, why? Was he somehow involved in her disappearance? Cruise officials said he passed a lie detector test. But why would the teenage witnesses lie?

18 The Bradley family did everything they could to find Amy. They hired private detectives. They made trips back to the Caribbean themselves. They even offered a $260,000 reward for Amy's safe return. Nothing worked.

19 As time passed, many people feared Amy was dead. The Bradleys refused to give up hope. But officials had run out of ideas. So Amy Bradley remains on the missing persons' list. And Amy's family is left with many haunting questions, but no good answers.

If you have been timed while reading this article, enter your reading time below. Then turn to the Words-per-Minute Table on page 101 and look up your reading speed (words per minute). Enter your reading speed on the graph on page 102.

Reading Time: Lesson 6

_____ : _____
Minutes   Seconds

A | Finding the Main Idea

One statement below expresses the main idea of the article. One statement is too general, or too broad. The other statement explains only part of the article; it is too narrow. Label the statements using the following key:

M—Main Idea   **B—Too Broad**   **N—Too Narrow**

_____ 1. Amy Bradley disappeared from a cruise ship on March 24, 1998, and investigators have been unable to discover what happened to her.

_____ 2. No one knows what happened to Amy Bradley on the morning of March 24, 1998.

_____ 3. A police trainee in Puerto Rico claimed to have seen Amy Bradley four days after she disappeared from the cruise ship.

_____ Score 15 points for a correct M answer.

_____ Score 5 points for each correct B or N answer.

_____ **Total Score:** Finding the Main Idea

B | Recalling Facts

How well do you remember the facts in the article? Put an X in the box next to the answer that correctly completes each statement about the article.

1. While she was on the cruise ship, Amy
   - ☐ a. gambled in the ship's casino.
   - ☐ b. went swimming in the ocean.
   - ☐ c. talked to many of the ship's crew members.

2. Amy's father last saw her
   - ☐ a. in the ship's disco.
   - ☐ b. talking to the band member Yellow.
   - ☐ c. on the balcony outside the family's cabin.

3. The F.B.I. did not think Amy had run away because she
   - ☐ a. was afraid of the ocean water.
   - ☐ b. seemed to have nothing to run away from.
   - ☐ c. seemed to be enjoying the cruise.

4. Supposedly Amy was last seen by
   - ☐ a. a police trainee in Puerto Rico.
   - ☐ b. two teenage girls.
   - ☐ c. her father.

5. When the Bradley family returned to the United States, they
   - ☐ a. hired private detectives to look for Yellow.
   - ☐ b. offered a big reward for Amy's return.
   - ☐ c. gave up their search for Amy.

Score 5 points for each correct answer.

_____ **Total Score:** Recalling Facts

C | Making Inferences

When you combine your own experience with information from a text to draw a conclusion that is not directly stated in that text, you are making an inference. Below are five statements that may or may not be inferences based on information in the article. Label the statements using the following key:

C—Correct Inference   F—Faulty Inference

_____ 1. Yellow was the last person on the cruise ship to see Amy Bradley.

_____ 2. Amy made friends easily.

_____ 3. The crew of the ship didn't want other passengers to know that someone had disappeared.

_____ 4. Amy left the cabin on the morning of March 24th because she couldn't sleep.

_____ 5. Amy was on the ship until March 28th when it stopped in Puerto Rico.

Score 5 points for each correct answer.

_____ **Total Score:** Making Inferences

D | Using Words Precisely

Each numbered sentence below contains an underlined word or phrase from the article. Following the sentence are three definitions. One definition is closest to the meaning of the underlined word. One definition is opposite or nearly opposite. Label those two definitions using the following key; do not label the remaining definition.

C—Closest   O—Opposite or Nearly Opposite

1. One of these new <u>acquaintances</u> was a band member on the ship.

_____ a. strangers

_____ b. friends

_____ c. co-workers

2. Brad and Amy went dancing in the ship's disco after enjoying a <u>formal</u> dinner with their parents.

_____ a. casual

_____ b. large

_____ c. fancy

3. Figuring she had fallen asleep out there, he saw no reason to <u>rouse her</u>.

_____ a. let her sleep

_____ b. awaken her

_____ c. talk to her

4. <u>Perplexed</u>, he decided to go up to the main deck to look for her.

_____ a. confused

_____ b. knowingly

_____ c. surprised

5. If someone had <u>nabbed</u> her, where had she been hidden?

_____ a. left

_____ b. seen

_____ c. taken

_____ Score 3 points for each correct C answer.

_____ Score 2 points for each correct O answer.

_____ **Total Score:** Using Words Precisely

Enter the four total scores in the spaces below, and add them together to find your Reading Comprehension Score. Then record your score on the graph on page 103.

Score	Question Type	Lesson 6
_____	Finding the Main Idea	
_____	Recalling Facts	
_____	Making Inferences	
_____	Using Words Precisely	
_____	**Reading Comprehension Score**	

Author's Approach

Put an X in the box next to the correct answer.

1. The main purpose of the first paragraph is to

☐ a. describe Amy Bradley.

☐ b. introduce the setting of the story.

☐ c. give details about Amy's disappearance.

2. What is the authors' purpose in writing "What Happened to Amy?"?

☐ a. to persuade the reader that Amy is still alive

☐ b. to inform the reader about Amy's situation

☐ c. to describe Amy and her family

3. The authors tell this story mainly by

☐ a. using their imagination and creativity.

☐ b. giving their opinions about the situation.

☐ c. retelling the experiences of the Bradley family.

_____ Number of correct answers

Record your personal assessment of your work on the Critical Thinking Chart on page 104.

CRITICAL THINKING

Summarizing and Paraphrasing

Follow the directions provided for questions 1 and 2. Put an X in the box next to the correct answer for question 3.

1. Look for the important ideas and events in paragraphs 7 and 8. Summarize those paragraphs in one or two sentences.

_____

_____

_____

2. Complete the following one-sentence summary of the article using the lettered phrases from the phrase bank below. Write the letters on the lines.

> **Phrase bank:**
> a. how she disappeared
> b. a description of what was done to find her
> c. a description of Amy

The article about Amy Bradley's disappearance begins with

_____, goes on to explain _____, and ends with

_____.

3. Choose the sentence that correctly restates the following sentence from the article: "The first two days of the cruise went smoothly."

☐ a. The Bradleys had a good time the first two days of the cruise.

☐ b. There were no problems the first two days of the cruise.

☐ c. The waters were calm the first two days of the cruise.

> _____ Number of correct answers
>
> Record your personal assessment of your work on the Critical Thinking Chart on page 104.

Critical Thinking

Put an X in the box next to the correct answer for questions 1, 2, and 5. Follow the directions provided for the other questions.

1. Which of the following statements from the article is an opinion rather than a fact?

☐ a. They thought Amy might be in someone's cabin or off in some little-used part of the ship.

☐ b. For three days planes and boats looked for Amy.

☐ c. No body was found in the waters around Curacao.

2. Based on the information in the article, you can predict that

☐ a. Amy Bradley will be found soon.

☐ b. Amy Bradley is in Puerto Rico.

☐ c. Amy Bradley's family will continue looking for her.

3. Which paragraphs provide evidence from the article to support your answer to question 2?

_____

4. Choose from the letters below to correctly complete the following statement. Write the letters on the lines.

According to paragraph 6, _____ because _____.

a. Mr. Bradley looked for a note from Amy

b. Mr. Bradley woke up

c. he heard someone leave the cabin

5. Into which of the following theme categories would this story fit?

☐ a. mystery

☐ b. drama

☐ c. romance

_____ Number of correct answers

Record your personal assessment of your work on the Critical Thinking Chart on page 104.

Personal Response

How do you think Brad Bradley felt when his sister disappeared?

_____

_____

_____

_____

Self-Assessment

From reading this article, I have learned

_____

_____

_____

_____

CRITICAL THINKING

Mysterious Circles

¹One morning in 1976 a farm worker in Hampshire, England, saw a strange sight. There was an odd circle in a field near highway A34. When the man checked it out, he grew even more puzzled. A perfectly round section of the field had been flattened. The stalks of grain were bent over in a swirling pattern. There were no footprints around. There was no sign that anyone had walked, run, or driven through the field.

2   Word of this mysterious "crop circle" spread quickly. Soon people spotted similar circles in other fields.

These complex crop circles were found in a wheat field in England.

The circles were most often found where some kind of grain was growing. But once in a while they appeared in other places. For instance, they were found among sugar beets. They were also found among soybeans and potato plants. Most of the circles were quite large. They might be 50 or 100 feet in diameter. A few were even bigger than football fields.

3 Most of the circles appeared in southern England. But some were found as far away as New Zealand and Japan. There was really no telling when or where the next crop circle was going to pop up. The circles always appeared within the space of a few hours. At twilight a field would look perfectly ordinary. By the next morning, there would be a big circle stamped on it. Once in a while, neighbors reported hearing a humming noise in the night. A few claimed they saw a bright light. But most of the time they noticed nothing at all.

4 Sometimes the crop circle was just that—a circle. On occasion, though, it was more complex. The design might feature a small circle inside a larger ring. There might be several circles side by side. Once in a while the circles had long lines that looked like tails. A few of the circles were found inside rectangles or other shapes.

5 At first skeptics thought the crop circles were a joke. They figured somebody was going out into fields and stomping on crops. But it wasn't that simple. To be sure, a few pranksters did make their own circles. But these fake ones were easy to spot. Footprints could be seen around the edges of the fake circles. The crop would be trampled and pushed into the ground wherever someone's boots had stepped.

6 With real crop circles, though, there were not any footprints. This was true even in muddy fields where it was impossible to walk without leaving tracks. One circle was seen on a snow-covered mountain in Afghanistan. There were no crops there. But the snow was packed down in the same swirling pattern. And not a single footprint led to or from the site.

7 When researchers began studying the circles, they discovered another interesting fact. There was evidence that crop circles had actually been around since well before 1976. Several books from the Middle Ages mention them. Many ancient stone carvings look similar to the shapes in the fields. If they are a joke, it's one that has been around for a long time.

8 A Scottish professor studying the circles explained why he didn't think they were hoaxes. "The crops around them are not disturbed at all," he said, "and the patterns are formed too perfectly."

9 Some people thought animals were making the circles. They thought hedgehogs could be the culprits. Hedgehogs do run in wild circles when they are mating. But that would not explain the absence of tracks. And it wouldn't explain how circles were made in rice paddies and other places where no hedgehogs live.

10 A few people thought helicopters might be to blame. If a helicopter hovered over a field, the wind from its rotors might flatten the crops. But that theory did not work, either. The circles often appeared in places

where no helicopters had been flying.

11 The more scientists studied the crop circles, the deeper the mystery got. They found that the circles did not kill the crops. In fake circles, the plants were trampled and broken. But in real ones, the plants were simply bent. It is quite easy to bend young plants. But as plants get older they become less flexible. It was hard to imagine how anyone could have bent fully-grown crops without destroying them.

12 One scientist spent years looking at crop circles. He found some made from stalks an inch thick. These stalks would snap if he tried to bend them more than 20 or 30 degrees. Yet in the crop circles these stalks were bent right over to the ground. He said, "I found many stems bent 120 degrees without the slightest snapping or splitting."

13 In the 1980s, another scientist came up with a new theory. He thought the circles might be formed by whirlwinds, or "spinning balls of air." He believed these balls became charged with electricity. When they touched the ground, they somehow shocked the plants. That caused the plants to bend.

14 Then another bizarre fact emerged. A scientist studying the cells of crop circle plants found that the cells were not normal. They were long and stretched out. When plants were grown from these seeds, the results were funny-shaped plants that grew bigger and quicker than they should have. The researcher agreed with the theory that whirlwinds created the circles, but believed the whirlwinds were full of microwave energy. These microwaves could heat the plants. That could make them soft enough to bend. The microwaves could also change the shape of the plants' cells.

15 Still, no one could say where the whirlwinds were coming from or how they were made. And to some people, the idea of whirlwinds did not make sense anyway. These people began to look for different answers. They wondered if crop circles were the work of aliens. They thought UFOs might be making the circles.

16 Many researchers did not believe this theory, but without another explanation, it was hard to rule it out. "This could be beyond science," admitted one scientist, who claimed to be skeptical about UFOs. "A very high level of intelligence is in control here."

17 To this day, no one knows what causes crop circles. But they keep coming. Every summer hundreds of them appear without warning. So who knows? Maybe it's just one of those mysteries that keeps going around and around.

If you have been timed while reading this article, enter your reading time below. Then turn to the Words-per-Minute Table on page 101 and look up your reading speed (words per minute). Enter your reading speed on the graph on page 102.

Reading Time: Lesson 7

_____ : _____
Minutes   *Seconds*

A Finding the Main Idea

One statement below expresses the main idea of the article. One statement is too general, or too broad. The other statement explains only part of the article; it is too narrow. Label the statements using the following key:

M—Main Idea   B—Too Broad   N—Too Narrow

_____ 1. Strange circles have appeared in fields in England and around the world, and no one knows what is causing them.

_____ 2. Some crop circles are bigger than a football field.

_____ 3. Crop circles are patterns of flattened crops or snow that appear mysteriously.

_____ Score 15 points for a correct M answer.

_____ Score 5 points for each correct B or N answer.

_____ **Total Score:** Finding the Main Idea

B Recalling Facts

How well do you remember the facts in the article? Put an X in the box next to the answer that correctly completes each statement about the article.

1. Crop circles are most often found
   ☐ a. in fields of soybeans.
   ☐ b. near highways.
   ☐ c. where grain is growing.

2. The crop circles are generally created
   ☐ a. overnight.
   ☐ b. as a joke.
   ☐ c. by hedgehogs.

3. Researchers do not think the circles are hoaxes because
   ☐ a. they appear all over the world.
   ☐ b. they don't know how the circles are made.
   ☐ c. the patterns are formed too perfectly.

4. The cells of plants in the crop circles are
   ☐ a. long and stretched out.
   ☐ b. bent.
   ☐ c. charged with electricity.

5. According to researchers, people have been seeing crop circles
   ☐ a. since 1976.
   ☐ b. since ancient times.
   ☐ c. when there are UFOs in the area.

Score 5 points for each correct answer.

_____ **Total Score:** Recalling Facts

C Making Inferences

When you combine your own experience with information from a text to draw a conclusion that is not directly stated in that text, you are making an inference. Below are five statements that may or may not be inferences based on information in the article. Label the statements using the following key:

C—Correct Inference   F—Faulty Inference

_____ 1. There were not many crop circle sightings in recent times before 1976.

_____ 2. The crop circles are being made by something that is shaped like a circle.

_____ 3. Crop circles cannot be made during the day.

_____ 4. Charging a plant with electricity causes it to become soft.

_____ 5. It does not take long to make a crop circle.

Score 5 points for each correct answer.

_____ **Total Score:** Making Inferences

D Using Words Precisely

Each numbered sentence below contains an underlined word or phrase from the article. Following the sentence are three definitions. One definition is closest to the meaning of the underlined word. One definition is opposite or nearly opposite. Label those two definitions using the following key; do not label the remaining definition.

C—Closest   O—Opposite or Nearly Opposite

1. The stalks of grain were bent over in a <u>swirling</u> pattern.

_____ a. straight

_____ b. circular

_____ c. flattened

2. At <u>twilight</u> a field would look perfectly ordinary.

_____ a dusk

_____ b. night

_____ c. dawn

3. On occasion, though, it was more <u>complex</u>.

_____ a. square

_____ b. complicated

_____ c. simple

4. At first, <u>skeptics</u> thought the crop circles were a joke.

_____ a. believers

_____ b. scientists

_____ c. critics

5. A Scottish professor studying the circles explained why he didn't think they were <u>hoaxes</u>.

_____ a. genuine

_____ b. fakes

_____ c. man-made

_____ Score 3 points for each correct C answer.

_____ Score 2 points for each correct O answer.

_____ **Total Score:** Using Words Precisely

Enter the four total scores in the spaces below, and add them together to find your Reading Comprehension Score. Then record your score on the graph on page 103.

Score	Question Type	Lesson 7
_____	Finding the Main Idea	
_____	Recalling Facts	
_____	Making Inferences	
_____	Using Words Precisely	
_____	**Reading Comprehension Score**	

Author's Approach

Put an X in the box next to the correct answer.

1. What is the authors' purpose in writing "Mysterious Circles"?

☐ a. to entertain the reader

☐ b. to encourage the reader to study crop circles

☐ c. to inform the reader about crop circles

2. The authors use the first sentence of the article to

☐ a. get the reader's attention.

☐ b. entertain the reader.

☐ c. inform the reader about crop circles.

3. The authors' opinion about crop circles is

☐ a. that they are made by whirlwinds.

☐ b. that they are made by UFOs.

☐ c. not stated in the article.

_____ Number of correct answers

Record your personal assessment of your work on the Critical Thinking Chart on page 104.

Summarizing and Paraphrasing

Follow the directions provided for questions 1 and 2. Put an X in the box next to the correct answer for question 3.

1. Look for the important ideas and events in paragraphs 5 and 6. Summarize those paragraphs in one or two sentences.

_____

_____

_____

2. Reread paragraph 14 in the article. Below, write a summary of the paragraph in no more than 25 words.

_____

_____

_____

_____

Reread your summary and decide whether it covers the important ideas in the paragraph. Next, decide how to shorten the summary to 15 words or less without leaving out any essential information. Write this summary below.

_____

_____

_____

3. Choose the sentence that correctly restates the following sentence from the article: "There was really no telling when or where the next crop circle was going to pop up."

☐ a. No one could predict when or where the next crop circle would appear.

☐ b. No one would tell when or where the next crop circle would appear.

☐ c. No one knew when the grain in a crop circle would pop back up.

_____ Number of correct answers

Record your personal assessment of your work on the Critical Thinking Chart on page 104.

Critical Thinking

Put an X in the box next to the correct answer for questions 1 and 2. Follow the directions provided for the other questions.

1. Which of the following statements from the article is an opinion rather than a fact?

☐ a. Once in a while the circles had long lines that looked like tails.

☐ b. In the 1980s, Terrence Meaden came up with a new theory.

☐ c. If a helicopter hovered over a field, the wind from its rotors might flatten the crops.

CRITICAL THINKING

2. From the information in the article, you can predict that

☐ a. scientists will continue studying crop circles.

☐ b. scientists will discover that crop circles are made by UFOs.

☐ c. crop circles will stop appearing.

3. Which paragraphs provide evidence from the article to support your answer to question 2?

_____

4. Using what you know about crop circles and the information in the article, list at least two ways fake crop circles are different from real ones.

_____

_____

_____

_____ Number of correct answers

Record your personal assessment of your work on the Critical Thinking Chart on page 104.

Personal Response

What was most surprising or interesting to you about this article?

_____

_____

_____

_____

Self-Assessment

Before reading this article, I already knew

_____

_____

_____

_____

Cuban Stowaway

Armando Socarras survived nine hours in a wheel well similar to this one on a flight from Cuba to Madrid, Spain.

[1]Twenty-two-year-old Armando Socarras wanted to leave Cuba. So did his 16-year-old friend Jorge Perez. They opposed Cuba's government and thought they could find more freedom and opportunity in Europe or the United States. Other Cubans felt the same way. Many had already fled their island nation in the Caribbean Sea. Most did it by boat. Socarras and Perez tried a different approach.

2   On June 4, 1969, the two young men went to the airport in Havana, Cuba. They hid in the tall grass near

the runway. A passenger jet was about to take off for a nine-hour flight to Madrid, Spain. Socarras and Perez didn't have tickets for the flight. Instead, they planned to be stowaways.

3   Socarras and Perez knew they couldn't sneak into the plane. So they planned to hide on the *outside* of the plane. Every jet has two big wheel wells. These are spaces on the underside of the plane's body. During flight, the wheels are tucked up into these wells. Socarras and Perez thought they could squeeze into one of the wheel wells and ride there all the way to Spain.

4   When no one was looking, they ran out onto the runway and climbed into the right wheel well. Then they hung on for dear life as the jet took off.

5   Once the plane was in the air the pilot pushed a lever. That lifted the wheels up into their wells. But something was wrong. The pilot saw his control light flickering. That meant the wheels were not fully closed within the wells. The pilot thought something might be stuck,

so he lowered the wheels again. When he raised them a second time, the control light went out. The wheels were now fully closed within the well, and the pilot thought nothing more about it.

6   Back in the wheel well, Socarras and Perez found the wheels pressed up against them. They had little space to move. But that was the least of their problems. Both of them were lightly dressed. Socarras wore just a cotton shirt and pants. As the jet climbed, the air grew much colder. By the time the plane reached 30,000 feet the temperature had dropped to 40 degrees below zero! "Little by little I felt cold, sleepy, and had great pains in my ears," Socarras later said. "I must have fallen asleep. I don't know anything more. I know that I woke up once thinking it was terribly cold."

7   Amazingly, though, Socarras made it. When the plane came to a stop, he fell out of the wheel well. He was unconscious. His clothes were coated with ice. Somewhere along the way he had lost a shoe. His hands, arms, and legs were frostbitten. But he was alive.

Jorge Perez was not so lucky. Socarras said that he rode with him throughout the flight, but Perez was not in the wheel well when the plane landed in Madrid. It is believed that he fell out when the pilot lowered the wheels to land.

8   When airport workers found Socarras, they rushed him to the hospital. Doctors soaked his frostbitten limbs in warm water. A short time later, Socarras regained consciousness. Except for signs of exposure and shock, he was in fairly good shape.

9   No one could believe it. The chief engineer for the company that had built the jet called Socarras's survival "a miracle." He pointed out that there was very little room in the wheel well. He said there was "one chance in a million" that the wheels wouldn't crush someone to death when they were pulled in.

10   Doctors, meanwhile, were stunned by the medical aspects of the case. They wondered how Socarras had survived without an oxygen mask. There is oxygen at 30,000 feet. But

there isn't much. There is only about one-fourth the amount found at sea level. Mountain climbers use bottled oxygen when they go above 25,000 feet. A few climbers go higher without it. But they spend weeks getting their bodies used to the thin air.

11 Then there was the lack of air pressure. The 143 people inside the jet rode in comfort because the cabin was pressurized. But Socarras was out in the open. Air pressure at 30,000 feet is only one-third of what it is at sea level. A rapid drop in air pressure causes gas bubbles to form in the blood. The result is a bad case of the "bends." Getting the bends can lead to paralysis and even death. No one could understand how Socarras had avoided this fate.

12 Finally there was the cold air. Socarras had spent hours in air that was 40 degrees below zero. And he had done it dressed just in light cotton clothes. When he got to Spain, his body temperature had dropped to 93 degrees. That's almost six degrees below normal.

13 Without doubt, the combination of little oxygen, low air pressure, and severe cold should have killed him. The human body is not built to survive such great extremes. The doctors could not explain it. Said one, "Very few human hearts, if any, have endured what [Socarras's] heart did."

14 In the end, some doctors thought Socarras might have survived the lack of oxygen *because* of the extreme cold. When a human body cools down, it needs less and less oxygen. Everything starts shutting down. The heart pumps more slowly. The lungs take in less air. If the cooling happens at just the right speed, a person might live. One doctor said that if Socarras had been chilled too fast, it would have been fatal. But if his body cooled gradually, its demand for oxygen could have kept up with the supply. In other words, he wouldn't need much oxygen because he was almost frozen.

15 Everyone agreed that Socarras was very lucky to be alive. Since 1969, many other people have fled Cuba. But it is no surprise that none have copied Socarras's means of escape. As one doctor said, "[riding in the wheel well of a jet] is not likely to become a popular way to travel."

If you have been timed while reading this article, enter your reading time below. Then turn to the Words-per-Minute Table on page 101 and look up your reading speed (words per minute). Enter your reading speed on the graph on page 102.

Reading Time: Lesson 8

_____ : _____

Minutes   Seconds

A Finding the Main Idea

One statement below expresses the main idea of the article. One statement is too general, or too broad. The other statement explains only part of the article; it is too narrow. Label the statements using the following key:

M—Main Idea   **B—Too Broad**   **N—Too Narrow**

_____ 1. There is very little extra room in the wheel well of a jet.

_____ 2. Armando Socarras survived nine hours in the wheel well of a jet in spite of freezing temperatures, low oxygen levels, and low air pressure.

_____ 3. Armando Socarras and Jorge Perez left Cuba in an unusual and dangerous way.

_____ Score 15 points for a correct M answer.

_____ Score 5 points for each correct B or N answer.

_____ **Total Score:** Finding the Main Idea

B Recalling Facts

How well do you remember the facts in the article? Put an X in the box next to the answer that correctly completes each statement about the article.

1. Armando Socarras and Jorge Perez decided to leave Cuba by
   - ☐ a. boat.
   - ☐ b. sneaking into a jet.
   - ☐ c. riding in the wheel well of a jet.

2. By the time the plane reached 30,000 feet,
   - ☐ a. Socarras and Perez had little room to move.
   - ☐ b. the temperature had dropped to 40 degrees below 0.
   - ☐ c. Socarras and Perez were lightly dressed.

3. When airport workers found Socarras,
   - ☐ a. they rushed him to the hospital.
   - ☐ b. they soaked his frostbitten limbs in warm water.
   - ☐ c. he was inside the wheel well of the plane.

4. Doctors were amazed that Socarras had
   - ☐ a. not worn warmer clothes.
   - ☐ b. survived without an oxygen mask.
   - ☐ c. frostbite.

5. Doctors thought Socarras might have survived because
   - ☐ a. of the lack of oxygen.
   - ☐ b. he was lucky.
   - ☐ c. his body cooled down slowly.

Score 5 points for each correct answer.

_____ **Total Score:** Recalling Facts

C | Making Inferences

When you combine your own experience with information from a text to draw a conclusion that is not directly stated in that text, you are making an inference. Below are five statements that may or may not be inferences based on information in the article. Label the statements using the following key:

C—Correct Inference   F—Faulty Inference

_____ 1. The Cuban government would not allow Socarras and Perez to leave the country.

_____ 2. Socarras and Perez were not very large.

_____ 3. Jorge Perez died during the flight to Madrid.

_____ 4. Socarras and Perez did not know all the risks of flying in the wheel well of a jet.

_____ 5. Socarras and Perez had relatives in Spain.

Score 5 points for each correct answer.

_____ **Total Score:** Making Inferences

D | Using Words Precisely

Each numbered sentence below contains an underlined word or phrase from the article. Following the sentence are three definitions. One definition is closest to the meaning of the underlined word. One definition is opposite or nearly opposite. Label those two definitions using the following key; do not label the remaining definition.

C—Closest   O—Opposite or Nearly Opposite

1. They <u>opposed</u> Cuba's government.

_____ a. supported

_____ b. fought

_____ c. disagreed with

2. No one could understand how Socarras had <u>avoided</u> this fate.

_____ a. escaped

_____ b. found

_____ c. thought about

3. The human body is not built to survive such great <u>extremes</u>.

_____ a. temperatures

_____ b. variations

_____ c. moderation

4. If Socarras had been chilled too fast, it would have been <u>fatal</u>.

_____ a. deadly

_____ b. dangerous

_____ c. life-giving

5. But through <u>gradual</u> cooling his body's demand for oxygen could have kept up with the supply.

_____ a. rapid

_____ b. continuous

_____ c. slow

_____ Score 3 points for each correct C answer.

_____ Score 2 points for each correct O answer.

_____ **Total Score:** Using Words Precisely

Enter the four total scores in the spaces below, and add them together to find your Reading Comprehension Score. Then record your score on the graph on page 103.

Score	Question Type	Lesson 8
_____	Finding the Main Idea	
_____	Recalling Facts	
_____	Making Inferences	
_____	Using Words Precisely	
_____	**Reading Comprehension Score**	

Author's Approach

Put an X in the box next to the correct answer.

1. The main purpose of the first paragraph is to
   - ☐ a. get the reader's attention.
   - ☐ b. give the reader background information for the story.
   - ☐ c. describe Armando Socarras and Jorge Perez.

2. What is the authors' purpose in writing "Cuban Stowaway"?
   - ☐ a. to discourage people from traveling in the wheel wells of jets
   - ☐ b. to describe Socarras's escape
   - ☐ c. to describe the effects on the human body of being 30,000 feet in the air

3. What do the authors imply by saying, "It is no surprise that [no one else has] copied Socarras's means of escape"?
   - ☐ a. Airports now check the wheel wells of jets to make sure no one is hiding there.
   - ☐ b. It is difficult to survive a flight in the wheel well of a jet.
   - ☐ c. It is risky to ride in the wheel well of a jet, and few people want to try it.

_____ Number of correct answers

Record your personal assessment of your work on the Critical Thinking Chart on page 104.

Summarizing and Paraphrasing

Follow the directions provided for questions 1 and 2. Put an X in the box next to the correct answer for question 3.

1. Look for the important ideas and events in paragraphs 6 and 7. Summarize those paragraphs in one or two sentences.

_____

_____

_____

2. Combine the lettered phrases in the phrase bank below into a one-sentence summary of the article. Write the summary on the lines below.

```
Phrase bank:
a.  in the wheel well of a jet
b.  from Cuba to Madrid, Spain
c.  a Cuban man
d.  miraculously survived a trip
```

_____

_____

_____

3. Read the statement from the article below. Then read the paraphrase of that statement. Choose the reason that best tells why the paraphrase does not say the same thing as the statement.

   Statement: "The doctors, meanwhile, were stunned by the medical aspects of the case."

   Paraphrase: The doctors were surprised that Socarras had survived the trip.

   ☐ a. Paraphrase says too much.

   ☐ b. Paraphrase doesn't say enough.

   ☐ c. Paraphrase doesn't agree with the statement about the article.

   _____ Number of correct answers

   Record your personal assessment of your work on the Critical Thinking Chart on page 104.

Critical Thinking

Put an X in the box next to the correct answer for questions 3 and 5. Follow the directions provided for the other questions.

1. For each statement below, write *O* if it expresses an opinion or *F* if it expresses a fact.

   _____ a. Air pressure at 30,000 feet is only one-third of what it is at sea level.

   _____ b. It is believed that he fell out when the pilot lowered the wheels to land.

   _____ c. If the cooling happens at just the right speed, a person might live.

2. Choose from the letters below to correctly complete the following statement. Write the letters on the lines.

On the positive side, _____, but on the negative side, _____.

   a. Socarras survived his trip in the wheel well

   b. he was in pretty good shape

   c. his friend Jorge Perez did not

3. What was one of the effects of Socarras's spending hours in air that was 40°F below zero?

☐ a. Gas bubbles formed in his blood.

☐ b. He didn't get enough oxygen.

☐ c. His body temperature dropped almost six degrees.

4. Which paragraphs provide evidence from the article to support your answer to question 3?

_____

5. Into which of the following theme categories would this story fit?

☐ a. mystery

☐ b. adventure

☐ c. historical fiction

_____ Number of correct answers

Record your personal assessment of your work on the Critical Thinking Chart on page 104.

Personal Response

How do you think Socarras and Perez felt as the plane took off?

_____

_____

_____

_____

Self-Assessment

The part I found most difficult about the article was _____

_____.

I found this difficult because _____

_____.

A Living Fossil

[1]What would you say if someone claimed to have found a *live* dinosaur? You'd probably say he or she was crazy. Everyone knows the dinosaurs died out tens of millions of years ago. The only place you can find one these days is in a museum.

[2] So was Marjorie Courtney-Latimer crazy? In 1938, she was working at a museum in South Africa. Her job was to collect fish specimens. One day she got a call from a fisherman who had been helping her find different kinds of fish. He had just brought in a fresh load of fish and wanted to show it to

The coelacanth, pictured here, has been on the earth for more than 80 million years. Scientists had thought coelacanths were extinct until a live one was found off the coast of South Africa in 1938.

her. He thought it might contain some new specimens.

3   When Courtney-Latimer got to the dock, she spotted one very strange fish. It didn't look like anything she had seen before. It was blue and about five feet long. "[It was] the most beautiful fish I had ever seen," she wrote. But she had no idea what it was. Unfortunately, it was already dead. Still, she decided it was worth keeping. She wrapped it in rags soaked with formaldehyde. That didn't work well. The flesh quickly rotted away. All that remained was the skin and a few bones.

4   Back at the museum, Courtney-Latimer looked through her books to see if she could find out what the fish was. She could not believe what she learned. The strange fish looked just like a coelacanth. But that was impossible! The coelacanth had been extinct for 80 million years. It was wiped out long before the dinosaurs. Humans knew about it only because of fossils that had been found.

5   Still, Courtney-Latimer thought her fish could be a coelacanth. She told her boss about it. He said she must be mistaken. He said the fish was probably just a rock cod.

6   Courtney-Latimer refused to let the matter drop. She sent a detailed sketch to Professor J. L. B. Smith, an expert on fish. Smith was stunned. The sketch looked like a coelacanth to him. He came to see the remains for himself. That convinced him. He believed Courtney-Latimer really had found a fish that dated back 80 million years.

7   Smith wanted to get his hands on a second coelacanth. Then he could document the discovery. He could prove beyond any doubt that the prehistoric fish was still alive. He sent notices to fishing villages in many parts of the world. The notice described the coelacanth. This fish can be four or five feet long. It does not have regular flat fins. Instead, it has stumpy rounded lobes. These lobes are jointed. They are almost like arms and legs. The coelacanth also has a bony head, small sharp teeth, and heavy scales.

8   In the notice Smith offered a reward of 100 pounds. The money would be paid to anyone who caught a second coelacanth. For a very long time no one did. Then, in 1952, a fisherman pulled up an odd-looking fish off the coast of the Comoro Islands. He showed it to a friend who remembered Smith's notice.

9   Smith rushed to see the fish. It was indeed a coelacanth. Smith was so moved by the sight that he began to weep. This was the zoological find of the century. But it also raised questions. How could a fish that had been "dead" for so long reappear? All the coelacanth fossils were 80 million years old. If the species was still swimming around, why hadn't more recent remains been found?

10   Scientists think they have figured out the answer. Perhaps 80 million years ago the fish lived in regions where fossils could be left. Later, the fish moved to regions that didn't produce fossils. So it didn't leave a record that could be traced.

11   In addition, the fish lives deep down in the ocean. The one Smith saw had come from 600 feet below the surface. The species can live as far down as 2,000 feet. Most fishermen did not look for fish in such deep

waters. Once in a great while a local fisherman would come ashore with one. But they never realized what they had in their nets. They wanted to catch fish that could be sold for food. Since this fish had no useful flesh, it was seen as little more than a nuisance.

12   Since 1952, more than two hundred coelacanths have been caught. Sadly, none have lived more than a day. These fish can't survive in shallow water. They are used to living at the immense pressure found deep in the ocean. The lighter pressure at sea level kills them, often within just a few hours. Also, surface waters are much too warm for them.

13   The amazing story of this fish has one more chapter. Until recently, experts thought coelacanths lived in just one place. That was off the coast of the Comoro Islands. A few had been caught as far away as South Africa. But those were thought to be strays.

14   In 1998, however, marine biologist Mark Erdmann was in Indonesia with his wife. While shopping one day, his wife saw a strange creature in a wooden cart. It did not look like any fish she had ever seen. She told Erdmann about it. He took one

look and knew right away it was a coelacanth. But how could that be? These fish had never been seen east of Madagascar. Now here was one 6,000 miles away!

15   Erdmann later found out that fishermen in those parts caught two or three coelacanths a year. One day, he even saw one hauled ashore in a shark net. It was still alive. The fish lived for six hours. That gave Erdmann time to photograph and study it. It looked just like the ones found off the coast of Africa. The only difference was the color. The African ones were pale blue with white marks. This one was a mix of brown and gray.

16   Are there more surprises in store? No one knows. But scientists think there are only about 500 of these creatures left in the world. That's a very small number. It's so small, in fact, that the fish has been put on the endangered species list. As fishermen cast nets deeper and deeper into the ocean, they keep bringing up coelacanths. "[The fish] could disappear in the next 15 to 20 years," says one marine biologist.

17   So far, there has been no real effort made to save the coelacanth. People just don't seem to care. "It's [hard]

to get money to conserve an animal that you can't see, and which tourists can't pay to go and look at," says the biologist. He also notes that people love to save animals that are warm and furry. They don't always worry about animals that are wet and slimy.

18   That could spell doom for the coelacanth. Here is a fish that has survived more than 350 million years on its own. Yet it could be wiped out less than 100 years after its discovery by humans. Then the once "dead" fish really will be dead.

A   Finding the Main Idea

One statement below expresses the main idea of the article. One statement is too general, or too broad. The other statement explains only part of the article; it is too narrow. Label the statements using the following key:

M—Main Idea   B—Too Broad   N—Too Narrow

_____ 1. In 1938 Marjorie Courtney-Latimer found a coelacanth off the coast of South Africa.

_____ 2. The coelacanth is usually four or five feet long and has stumpy round lobes in place of fins.

_____ 3. In 1938 a scientist discovered that the coelacanth, which was thought to be extinct, still lives deep in the ocean.

_____ Score 15 points for a correct M answer.

_____ Score 5 points for each correct B or N answer.

_____ **Total Score:** Finding the Main Idea

B   Recalling Facts

How well do you remember the facts in the article? Put an X in the box next to the answer that correctly completes each statement about the article.

1. When Courtney-Latimer went to the dock in 1938, she
   ☐ a. immediately realized that the unusual fish she saw was a coelacanth.
   ☐ b. saw one fish that looked different from anything she'd seen before.
   ☐ c. noticed a strange, spotted fish.

2. Until 1938 scientists thought the coelacanth
   ☐ a. looked similar to a rock cod.
   ☐ b. had been extinct for 80 million years.
   ☐ c. had been wiped out by the dinosaurs.

3. Coelacanths live
   ☐ a. near the shores of the Comoro Islands.
   ☐ b. in shallow water.
   ☐ c. deep in the ocean.

4. The difference between the Indonesian and African coelacanth is that
   ☐ a. one is blue, and the other is brown and gray.
   ☐ b. the Indonesian one lives longer.
   ☐ c. the Indonesian one lives closer to the shore.

5. Coelacanths are in danger of dying out because
   ☐ a. they can't live in surface waters.
   ☐ b. fishermen are casting their nets deeper than they used to.
   ☐ c. fishermen can sell them for a good price.

Score 5 points for each correct answer.

_____ **Total Score:** Recalling Facts

C | Making Inferences

When you combine your own experience with information from a text to draw a conclusion that is not directly stated in that text, you are making an inference. Below are five statements that may or may not be inferences based on information in the article. Label the statements using the following key:

C—Correct Inference   F—Faulty Inference

_____ 1. The rock cod and the coelacanth look similar.

_____ 2. Coelacanths used to walk on land.

_____ 3. The coelacanth has difficulty adapting to changes in its environment.

_____ 4. Coelacanths are not good to eat.

_____ 5. Coelacanths do not reproduce in large numbers.

Score 5 points for each correct answer.

_____ **Total Score:** Making Inferences

D | Using Words Precisely

Each numbered sentence below contains an underlined word or phrase from the article. Following the sentence are three definitions. One definition is closest to the meaning of the underlined word. One definition is opposite or nearly opposite. Label those two definitions using the following key; do not label the remaining definition.

C—Closest   O—Opposite or Nearly Opposite

1. Then he could <u>document</u> the discovery.

_____ a. record

_____ b. ignore

_____ c. erase

2. Smith was so moved by the sight that he began to <u>weep</u>.

_____ a. scream

_____ b. laugh

_____ c. cry

3. Since this fish had no useful flesh, it was seen as little more than <u>a nuisance</u>.

_____ a. a pleasure

_____ b. an annoyance

_____ c. harmful

4. They are used to living at the <u>immense</u> pressure found deep in the ocean.

_____ a. weak

_____ b. large

_____ c. strong

5. It's [hard] to get money to <u>conserve</u> an animal that you can't
   see.

_____ a. save

_____ b. study

_____ c. destroy

_____ Score 3 points for each correct C answer.

_____ Score 2 points for each correct O answer.

_____ **Total Score:** Using Words Precisely

Enter the four total scores in the spaces below, and add them
together to find your Reading Comprehension Score. Then record
your score on the graph on page 103.

Score	Question Type	Lesson 9
_____	Finding the Main Idea	
_____	Recalling Facts	
_____	Making Inferences	
_____	Using Words Precisely	
_____	**Reading Comprehension Score**	

Author's Approach

Put an X in the box next to the correct answer.

1. The authors use the first sentence of the article to

☐ a. entertain the reader.

☐ b. describe the coelacanth.

☐ c. get the reader's attention.

2. What do the authors imply by saying, "people love to save
   animals that are warm and furry"?

☐ a. Bears are more popular animals than fish.

☐ b. People are more interested in saving animals they can see
   in a forest or zoo than animals that live out of sight.

☐ c. People like animals that live on land more than animals
   that live in the ocean.

3. Which of the following statements from the article best
   describes the coelacanth?

☐ a. It was blue and about five feet long.

☐ b. A fisherman pulled up an odd-looking fish off the coast of
   the Comoro Islands.

☐ c. It has stumpy round lobes, . . . a bony head, small sharp
   teeth, and heavy scales.

_____ Number of correct answers

Record your personal assessment of your work on the
Critical Thinking Chart on page 104.

Summarizing and Paraphrasing

Follow the directions provided for the questions below.

1. Look for the important ideas and events in paragraphs 3 and 4. Summarize those paragraphs in one or two sentences.

_____

_____

_____

2. Reread paragraph 14 in the article. Below, write a summary of the paragraph in no more than 25 words.

_____

_____

_____

_____

Reread your summary and decide whether it covers the important ideas in the paragraph. Next, decide how to shorten the summary to 15 words or less without leaving out any essential information. Write this summary below.

_____

_____

_____

3. Read the statement from the article below. Then read the paraphrase of that statement. Choose the reason that best tells why the paraphrase does not say the same thing as the statement.

    Statement: "The coelacanth had been extinct for 80 million years."

    Paraphrase: The coelacanth has been on the earth for 80 million years.

☐ a. Paraphrase says too much.

☐ b. Paraphrase doesn't say enough.

☐ c. Paraphrase doesn't agree with the statement from the article.

_____ Number of correct answers

Record your personal assessment of your work on the Critical Thinking Chart on page 104.

Critical Thinking

Put an X in the box next to the correct answer for question 1. Follow the directions provided for the other questions.

1. Which of the following statements from the article is an opinion rather than a fact?

☐ a. It was the most beautiful fish I had ever seen.

☐ b. She wrapped it in rags soaked in formaldehyde.

☐ c. They can live as far down as 2,000 feet.

2. Using the information in the article, list the ways the Indonesian coelacanth is different from the African coelacanth.

_____

_____

_____

3. In which paragraphs did you find the information to support your answer to question 2?

_____

4. Choose from the letters below to correctly complete the following statement. Write the letters on the lines.

According to paragraphs 9–11, _____ because

_____.

a. they moved to regions that didn't produce fossils

b. they live deep in the ocean

c. scientists thought coelacanths were extinct

_____ Number of correct answers

Record your personal assessment of your work on the Critical Thinking Chart on page 104.

Personal Response

How would you feel if you found an animal that was thought to be extinct?

_____

_____

_____

_____

Self-Assessment

One word or phrase in the article that I do not understand is

_____

_____

_____

_____

The 29,000-Foot Plunge

[1]Steve Fossett loved a challenge—any challenge. He had the time, money, and courage to take on even the most daring feats. A millionaire, Fossett wasn't about to stay home and count his money.

[2]   Over the years he tried just about every endurance test. He did not always set out to win or break a record. Sometimes he just wanted to prove he could do something. So he swam the English Channel. He raced with a team of dogs across Alaska. He

Steve Fossett flew more than 15,000 miles in his balloon, the Solo Spirit, before a storm caused him to crash into the ocean east of Australia. This photo was taken in a stadium in Argentina as Fossett was about to begin his trip.

competed in a 24-hour car race and ran in a 100-mile road race. When it came to ocean sailing, Fossett was one of the very best. He set eight long-distance records in that sport.

3   His greatest challenge, however, came in the air. Fossett wanted to fly nonstop around the world in a hot-air balloon. Others had tried to do this. So far, no one had made it. Weather or other problems always forced the balloonists to land. Fossett himself tried it five times. He never made it. In fact, on one trip he was lucky just to escape with his life.

4   In 1996, in his first attempt, Fossett traveled only 2,000 miles before he was forced to land. A year later he took off from St. Louis and made it halfway around the world to India. That trip covered more than 10,000 miles. At the time, it set a world record. In his third attempt Fossett again launched from St. Louis. Five days and 6,000 miles later, he came down in a wheat field in Russia. On August 7, 1998, he began his fourth flight. This was the one that almost killed him. For this fourth

flight Fossett launched his balloon, *Solo Spirit*, from South America. The 150-foot-high balloon headed east.

5   At first things went well. Fossett flew over the Atlantic Ocean. He crossed Africa and the Indian Ocean. He crossed Australia in record time. Nine days into the flight, Fossett had logged more than 15,200 miles. Everything had gone smoothly, and he thought this time he would really make it. When he was just five days from landing where he had started in Argentina, Fossett sent an e-mail message to his control center in St. Louis. "Things look good now," he said. "They'd better. Next land is South America. Cheers, Steve." That was the last message he sent.

6   About 500 miles east of Australia, Fossett ran into trouble. A line of thunderstorms suddenly appeared. He was flying at 29,000 feet. At that height he thought he could fly over the top of the storm. He was wrong. The fierce winds sucked him down into the heart of the storm. Although he was over a warm part of the earth, the temperature that high up was below

zero. So it didn't rain; it hailed. "[There were] tremendous sheets of hail just flooding me," Fossett later said. Also, bolts of lightning flashed all around.

7   Before long, the storm ripped a hole in Fossett's balloon. The *Solo Spirit* began to fall—fast. Within seconds it was falling at about 30 miles an hour. "I'm going to die," thought Fossett. As he plummeted, he kept running the burner full-tilt. It pumped hot air up into the damaged balloon. He knew that wouldn't stop the balloon from falling, but he hoped it would slow it down a bit. Still, it was a fearful plunge. "As I was going down," Fossett later said, "the balloon was just being thrown from one side to another."

8   Half a world away in St. Louis, his support crew knew nothing of Fossett's predicament. But they feared the worst. When they lost contact with him, they didn't know if he was still aloft. In fact, they didn't even know if he was still alive. Desperately they kept trying to reach him by radio. "In these situations, you just try to turn off your emotions," said team member Joe Ritchie.

9   When Fossett's balloon burst, he was over the Coral Sea. That was both a good and a bad place to land. It was good because the warm water was fairly shallow and protected by coral reefs, so he would not be tossed about by huge waves. "It's a lot better to [crash in the Coral Sea] than in the open Pacific," said one team member.

10   The bad part was that the coral reefs in this part of the ocean were uncharted. No one knew exactly where the reefs were. So rescuers ran the risk of hitting one. That could rip out the bottom of a boat. Also, the Coral Sea is home to the great white shark. If Fossett survived the 29,000-foot fall, he might still have to deal with these fearsome creatures.

11   Incredibly, Fossett did survive the fall. However, when he hit the water, he was knocked out. He also suffered small burns on his wrist and nose. When he woke up, Fossett realized that his capsule was upside down. Part of it was filling with water. Another part was on fire. Quickly Fossett climbed into a small life raft he had carried on board. As he pulled the life raft away from the capsule, the balloon's propane gas tanks exploded. Luckily, the blast didn't reach him.

12   Fossett's emergency beacon sent out a distress signal. That alerted ships and planes that he was in the area. Still, it took awhile for a search plane to locate him. The crew dropped a larger raft for him to wait in until he could be picked up. At last he was rescued by a ship that was on its own voyage around the world. The captain, Laurie Piper, had heard that Fossett was down and went looking for him. Somehow, she had managed to miss all the reefs while sailing in the dark!

13   The news that Fossett was safe delighted his team members back in St. Louis. "We've been sweating bullets for about eight hours," said one. "So we're feeling pretty good now."

14   Another agreed. "He is fortunate. There are not too many people who have been in a storm like that."

15   Steve Fossett survived his 29,000-foot plunge, but the *Solo Spirit* did not fare as well. The capsule was badly damaged, and most of the equipment was lost. That ruled out a second try in 1998. Fossett joined forces with another team. But their attempt in December also failed.

16   Soon there was no need to try anymore. In March 1999 the balloon *Breitling Orbiter 3* made a nonstop flight around the world. That trip, made by Brian Jones and Bertrand Piccard, took 19 days. It covered more than 29,000 miles, breaking all the records for such a flight. Steve Fossett would have to find a new challenge to test his skill and daring.

If you have been timed while reading this article, enter your reading time below. Then turn to the Words-per-Minute Table on page 101 and look up your reading speed (words per minute). Enter your reading speed on the graph on page 102.

Reading Time: Lesson 10

_____ : _____
Minutes   *Seconds*

A | Finding the Main Idea

One statement below expresses the main idea of the article. One statement is too general, or too broad. The other statement explains only part of the article; it is too narrow. Label the statements using the following key:

M—Main Idea   **B—Too Broad**   **N—Too Narrow**

_____ 1. In his fourth attempt to be the first person to fly nonstop around the world in a hot-air balloon, Steve Fossett crashed in a storm and nearly died.

_____ 2. Steve Fossett made five attempts to circle the earth in a hot-air balloon.

_____ 3. Steve Fossett ran into a storm about 500 miles east of Australia.

_____ Score 15 points for a correct M answer.

_____ Score 5 points for each correct B or N answer.

_____ **Total Score:** Finding the Main Idea

B | Recalling Facts

How How well do you remember the facts in the article? Put an X in the box next to the answer that correctly completes each statement about the article.

1. Steve Fossett began his balloon trip in the *Solo Spirit* in
☐ a. St. Louis.
☐ b. South America.
☐ c. Russia.

2. Fossett ran into trouble
☐ a. after logging about 29,000 miles.
☐ b. when he was five days away from completing his trip.
☐ c. when he was flying over Australia.

3. The *Solo Spirit* began to fall because
☐ a. fierce winds sucked it into the storm.
☐ b. it was caught in a hail storm.
☐ c. the storm ripped a hole in the balloon.

4. The Coral Sea was a good place for Fossett to land because
☐ a. its coral reefs were uncharted.
☐ b. the water was warm and protected by coral reefs.
☐ c. it had huge waves.

5. After the *Solo Spirit* crashed,
☐ a. Fossett did not want to fly a hot-air balloon again.
☐ b. it was damaged too badly to fly again that year.
☐ c. Fossett flew around the world in the *Breitling Orbiter 3*.

Score 5 points for each correct answer.

_____ **Total Score:** Recalling Facts

95

C | Making Inferences

When you combine your own experience with information from a text to draw a conclusion that is not directly stated in that text, you are making an inference. Below are five statements that may or may not be inferences based on information in the article. Label the statements using the following key:

C—Correct Inference   F—Faulty Inference

_____ 1. Steve Fossett was in good physical shape.

_____ 2. Storms usually occur below 29,000 feet.

_____ 3. The *Solo Spirit* was hit by lightning.

_____ 4. Fossett would have died if he had not regained consciousness when he did.

_____ 5. Fossett's next challenge would be learning to fly an airplane.

Score 5 points for each correct answer.

_____ **Total Score:** Making Inferences

D | Using Words Precisely

Each numbered sentence below contains an underlined word or phrase from the article. Following the sentence are three definitions. One definition is closest to the meaning of the underlined word. One definition is opposite or nearly opposite. Label those two definitions using the following key; do not label the remaining definition.

C—Closest   O—Opposite or Nearly Opposite

1. In 1996, Fossett traveled only 2,000 miles before he was <u>forced</u> to land.

_____ a. decided

_____ b. made to

_____ c. tried

2. Everything had gone <u>smoothly</u>, and he thought this time he would really make it.

_____ a. badly

_____ b. well

_____ c. quickly

3. As he <u>plummeted</u>, he kept running the burner full-tilt.

_____ a. fell

_____ b. rose

_____ c. moved

4. When they lost contact with him, they didn't know if he was still <u>aloft</u>.

_____ a. alive

_____ b. on the ground

_____ c. in the air

5. "We've been <u>sweating bullets</u> for about eight hours," said Joe Ritchie.

_____ a. very worried

_____ b. very warm

_____ c. calm

_____ Score 3 points for each correct C answer.

_____ Score 2 points for each correct O answer.

_____ **Total Score:** Using Words Precisely

Enter the four total scores in the spaces below, and add them together to find your Reading Comprehension Score. Then record your score on the graph on page 103.

Score	Question Type	Lesson 10
_____	Finding the Main Idea	
_____	Recalling Facts	
_____	Making Inferences	
_____	Using Words Precisely	
_____	**Reading Comprehension Score**	

Author's Approach

Put an X in the box next to the correct answer.

1. The main purpose of the first paragraph is to

☐ a. entertain the reader.

☐ b. describe Steve Fossett.

☐ c. describe some of the challenges Steve Fossett has undertaken.

2. Which of the following statements from the article best describes Steve Fossett?

☐ a. Over the years, he tried just about every endurance test.

☐ b. He did not always set out to break a record.

☐ c. Steve Fossett loved a challenge—any challenge.

3. Based on the statement from the article, "Steve Fossett would have to find a new challenge to test his skill and daring," you can conclude that the author wants the reader to think that

☐ a. Steve Fossett does not want to fly a balloon around the world if there is no record to break.

☐ b. Steve Fossett didn't want to fly a balloon again after the *Solo Spirit* crashed.

☐ c. Steve Fossett did not think ballooning was enough of a challenge any longer.

_____ Number of correct answers

Record your personal assessment of your work on the Critical Thinking Chart on page 104.

Summarizing and Paraphrasing

Follow the directions provided for questions 1 and 2. Put an X in the box next to the correct answer for question 3.

1. Look for the important ideas and events in paragraphs 6 and 7. Summarize those paragraphs in one or two sentences.

_____

_____

_____

_____

2. Complete the following one-sentence summary of the article using the lettered phrases from the phrase bank below. Write the letters on the lines.

> **Phrase bank:**
> a. what happened on his flight in the *Solo Spirit*
> b. a description of the first successful nonstop balloon flight around the world
> c. a description of Fossett and the feats he has attempted

The article about Steve Fossett begins with _____, goes on to explain _____, and ends with _____.

3. Choose the best one-sentence paraphrase for the following sentence from the article: "A millionaire, Fossett wasn't about to stay home and count his money."

☐ a. Fossett didn't like counting money.

☐ b. Fossett took advantage of his money and free time to undertake challenging sports.

☐ c. Fossett would rather go out and spend his money than stay home and save it.

> _____ Number of correct answers
>
> Record your personal assessment of your work on the Critical Thinking Chart on page 104.

Critical Thinking

Put an X in the box next to the correct answer for questions 1, 2, and 5. Follow the directions provided for the other questions.

1. Which of the following statements from the article is an opinion rather than a fact?

☐ a. He raced with a team of dogs across Alaska.

☐ b. Everything had gone smoothly, and he thought this time he would really make it.

☐ c. Nine days into the flight, Fossett had logged more than 15,200 miles.

2. From what the article told you about Steve Fossett, you can predict that

☐ a.   he will not ride in a hot-air balloon again.

☐ b.   he will continue to challenge himself with new, dangerous sports.

☐ c.   flying an airplane will be his next challenge.

3. Which paragraphs provide evidence from the article to support your answer to question 2?

_____

4. Choose from the letters below to correctly complete the following statement. Write the letters on the lines.

   According to paragraphs 11 and 12, _____ because

   _____.

   a.   the blast from the balloon's gas tanks didn't reach Fossett

   b.   he managed to climb into his life raft

   c.   Fossett sent out a distress signal

5. Into which of the following theme categories would this story fit?

☐ a.   adventure

☐ b.   mystery

☐ c.   historical fiction

_____
| _____ Number of correct answers

Record your personal assessment of your work on the Critical Thinking Chart on page 104.
_____

Personal Response

I wonder why

_____

_____

_____

_____

Self-Assessment

From reading this article, I have learned

_____

_____

_____

_____

Compare and Contrast

Think about the articles you have read in Unit Two. Pick the three articles you thought were the hardest to believe. Write the titles of the articles in the first column of the chart below. Use information you have learned from the articles to fill in the empty boxes in the chart.

Title	What is the most amazing thing you learned in this article?	What were people's reactions when they found out about the event in the article?	What was the effect of the event in the article on the people in the article?

Choose the person from one of these stories that you would most like to meet. Explain why you would like to meet him or her.

_____

_____

Words-per-Minute Table

Unit Two

Directions: If you were timed while reading an article, refer to the Reading Time you recorded in the box at the end of the article. Use this Words-per-Minute Table to determine your reading speed for that article. Then plot your reading speed on the graph on page 102.

Lesson	6	7	8	9	10	
No. of Words	1283	1051	1012	1175	1113	
1:30	855	701	675	783	742	**90**
1:40	770	631	607	705	668	**100**
1:50	700	573	552	641	607	**110**
2:00	642	526	506	588	557	**120**
2:10	592	485	467	542	514	**130**
2:20	550	450	434	504	477	**140**
2:30	513	420	405	470	445	**150**
2:40	481	394	380	441	417	**160**
2:50	453	371	357	415	393	**170**
3:00	428	350	337	392	371	**180**
3:10	405	332	320	371	351	**190**
3:20	385	315	304	353	334	**200**
3:30	367	300	289	336	318	**210**
3:40	350	287	276	320	304	**220**
3:50	335	274	264	307	290	**230**
4:00	321	263	253	294	278	**240**
4:10	308	252	243	282	267	**250**
4:20	296	243	234	271	257	**260**
4:30	285	234	225	261	247	**270**
4:40	275	225	217	252	239	**280**
4:50	265	217	209	243	230	**290**
5:00	257	210	202	235	223	**300**
5:10	248	203	196	227	215	**310**
5:20	241	197	190	220	209	**320**
5:30	233	191	184	214	202	**330**
5:40	226	185	179	207	196	**340**
5:50	220	180	173	201	191	**350**
6:00	214	175	169	196	186	**360**
6:10	208	170	164	191	180	**370**
6:20	203	166	160	186	176	**380**
6:30	197	162	156	181	171	**390**
6:40	192	158	152	176	167	**400**
6:50	188	154	148	172	163	**410**
7:00	183	150	145	168	159	**420**
7:10	179	147	141	164	155	**430**
7:20	175	143	138	160	152	**440**
7:30	171	140	135	157	148	**450**
7:40	167	137	132	153	145	**460**
7:50	164	134	129	150	142	**470**
8:00	160	131	127	147	139	**480**

Minutes and Seconds

Seconds

Plotting Your Progress: Reading Speed

Unit Two

Directions: If you were timed while reading an article, write your words-per-minute rate for that article in the box under the number of the lesson. Then plot your reading speed on the graph by putting a small X on the line directly above the number of the lesson, across from the number of words per minute you read. As you mark your speed for each lesson, graph your progress by drawing a line to connect the X's.

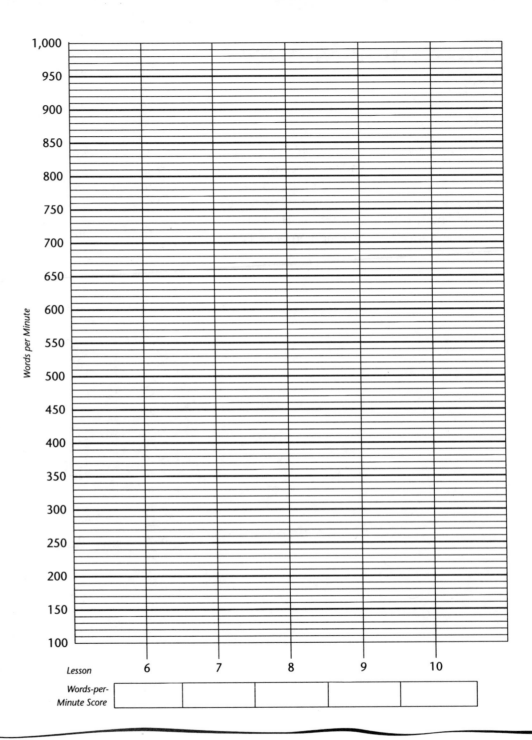

Plotting Your Progress: Reading Comprehension

Unit Two

Directions: Write your Reading Comprehension score for each lesson in the box under the number of the lesson. Then plot your score on the graph by putting a small X on the line directly above the number of the lesson and across from the score you earned. As you mark your score for each lesson, graph your progress by drawing a line to connect the X's.

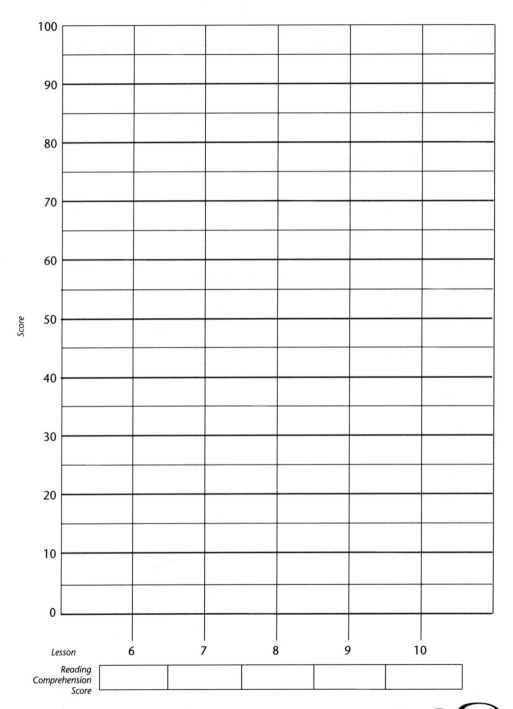

Plotting Your Progress: Critical Thinking

Unit Two

Directions: Work with your teacher to evaluate your responses to the Critical Thinking questions for each lesson. Then fill in the appropriate spaces in the chart below. For each lesson and each type of Critical Thinking question, do the following: Mark a minus sign (–) in the box to indicate areas in which you feel you could improve. Mark a plus sign (+) to indicate areas in which you feel you did well. Mark a minus-slash-plus sign (–/+) to indicate areas in which you had mixed success. Then write any comments you have about your performance, including ideas for improvement.

Lesson	Author's Approach	Summarizing and Paraphrasing	Critical Thinking
6			
7			
8			
9			
10			

UNIT THREE

A Guardian Angel?

[1]It was late in the day when Christene Skubish left Placerville, California. She buckled her three-year-old son Nicky into the passenger seat of her small red car. Then she set out to visit friends in Carson City, Nevada.

[2]   Sadly, Christene never made it. As she drove along Highway 50 on June 6, 1994, she must have fallen asleep at the wheel. She drove right off the road, leaving no skid marks at all. The car rolled 40 feet down a steep bank. It crashed into a thick forest of trees. Nicky was not badly hurt, but Christene was killed instantly.

Christene Skubish's car was destroyed when it plunged over the edge of a cliff along a California highway. Miraculously, her son Nicky survived the crash.

3   No one saw the accident take place. So Christene's friends had no idea why she and Nicky didn't arrive in Carson City as planned. For five days no one knew what had happened. During that time Nicky stayed near the body of his dead mother. He didn't know why she wouldn't wake up, but he didn't want to leave her. So even though he crawled out of the wrecked car from time to time, he didn't go far, and he eventually returned to the front seat to lie down beside her.

4   As the hours passed Nicky became hungry and thirsty. There was no food around for him to eat and nothing at all to drink. During the day the temperature rose into the 90s. Nicky got so hot he took off all his clothes. But at night the temperature plummeted back down to about 50 degrees. Because Nicky couldn't manage to get his clothes back on, he lay on the seat naked, shivering with cold. By the fourth night he was so weak he could barely move at all.

5   Meanwhile, Christene's friends and family were becoming more and more worried. They contacted the El Dorado County Sheriff's Department. Deputy Rich Strasser began to investigate but could find no leads.

6   Then, at 3 A.M. on June 11, a woman named Deborah Hoyt saw a bizarre sight. She and her husband were driving along Highway 50 on their way home from a trip. With her husband at the wheel, Deborah Hoyt was looking out the window. Suddenly she saw a naked woman lying by the side of the road. The woman was curled up in a ball, with one arm thrown across her head as though shielding her face.

7   "I just started screaming and screaming," Hoyt said. Her husband hadn't seen the woman, but he agreed they should get help right away. They stopped at a forest ranger's station two miles down the road and called the police.

8   When the highway police arrived, the Hoyts took them back to the spot where Deborah had seen the woman. There was no one there. The officers searched for an hour, covering a five-mile stretch of Highway 50. But they came up empty.

9   Yet Deborah Hoyt was absolutely certain about what she had seen. So at 5 A.M. that morning the officers put in a call to the El Dorado County Sheriff's office. They asked a local officer to follow up on Hoyt's strange sighting.

10   When Rich Strasser heard about the naked woman, he immediately thought of Christene Skubish. Deborah Hoyt's description of the naked woman matched that of Christene. So Deputy Strasser decided to drive out to Highway 50 himself and have a look around.

11   When he got out to the area where Hoyt had seen the woman, Strasser slowed down. The sun was just rising, and the road was deserted. As he crept along, Strasser saw no sign of a woman anywhere. But suddenly he spotted a small black object lying on the road. It was a child's hightop shoe.

12   Strasser pulled to a stop and jumped out of the car. He looked out over the steep bank. At first he saw nothing. Then, down among the trees, he saw the smashed remains of a red car.

13   With his heart pumping wildly, Strasser slid down the steep bank. He was hoping for a happy ending to the Skubish disappearance. But when he got to the car, he saw Christene's body

strapped in her seat. He also saw Nicky curled up beside her, blue and unmoving. It looked as though both of them were dead.

14   As Strasser bent over Nicky, however, he heard the little boy sigh. Nicky was alive! He couldn't believe Nicky had survived this long amid the wreckage. In fact, Nicky Skubish was on the verge of death. "He didn't talk or move, just lay there breathing," Strasser remembered. "The doctors who saw Nicky said if I hadn't found him when I did, he would have been dead within an hour."

15   After Nicky was rushed to the hospital, Strasser and others tried to piece together what had happened. But some of the facts simply did not make sense. Deborah Hoyt had seen a naked woman by the side of the road. But that woman could not have been Christene Skubish. Investigators were sure she had died in the crash. There were many deep cuts on her body that would have bled heavily. Very little blood had flowed out of these wounds, however, indicating that she had died instantly.

16   Besides, when Strasser found Christene, she was still in the driver's seat of her car with the seatbelt fastened. It didn't make sense to think that Christene had taken her clothes off, scrambled up the bank, collapsed by the side of the road, and then slid back down the bank, put her clothes back on, and buckled herself back into her seat before dying.

17   The naked person could not have been Nicky, either. "A healthy person would have had a very difficult time climbing up that embankment," said Strasser. "By the time Deborah Hoyt had seen someone, Nicky would have been too weak to move."

18   Then there was the matter of the black hightop shoe. No one could explain how it ended up in the middle of the road. If it had been there since the crash, why didn't the highway police officers find it when they searched the area? If Nicky had somehow managed to climb up the bank, it didn't make sense that he would carry one shoe up with him, drop the shoe in the middle of the road, and then slide down the bank again.

19   Finally, there were questions raised about Christene Skubish's body. It had not decayed at all. A body that had sat in 90-degree heat for five days should have been smelly and rotten. But Christene's body was in perfect shape. In fact, rescue workers noted a sweet smell surrounding it. "It's almost as though the condition of her body was preserved to make things easier for her son," mused Strasser. "In his mind, he thought his mom was just asleep."

20   In the end some people concluded that the naked woman was an angel. They said Nicky's guardian angel was guiding rescuers to his side. Others thought it was the spirit of Christene Skubish making one last attempt to save her son. But whoever or whatever it was, it saved the life of Nicky Skubish. If Deborah Hoyt had not seen the naked woman by the side of the road and gone for help, Nicky Skubish would not be alive today.

If you have been timed while reading this article, enter your reading time below. Then turn to the Words-per-Minute Table on page 147 and look up your reading speed (words per minute). Enter your reading speed on the graph on page 148.

Reading Time: Lesson 11

_____ : _____

Minutes   Seconds

A Finding the Main Idea

One statement below expresses the main idea of the article. One statement is too general, or too broad. The other statement explains only part of the article; it is too narrow. Label the statements using the following key:

M—Main Idea   B—Too Broad   N—Too Narrow

_____ 1. It is amazing that Nicky Skubish survived the crash that killed his mother.

_____ 2. It is still a mystery who the naked woman lying by the side of the road was and why Christene Skubish's body had not decayed after five days.

_____ 3. A black hightop shoe led Deputy Strasser to the place where Christene Skubish's car had crashed.

_____ Score 15 points for a correct M answer.

_____ Score 5 points for each correct B or N answer.

_____ **Total Score:** Finding the Main Idea

B Recalling Facts

How well do you remember the facts in the article? Put an X in the box next to the answer that correctly completes each statement about the article.

1. Nicky Skubish stayed near the wrecked car because he
   - [ ] a. couldn't climb up the steep hill.
   - [ ] b. didn't want to leave his mother.
   - [ ] c. was too weak to move.

2. While she and her husband were driving home, Deborah Hoyt saw
   - [ ] a. Christene Skubish's body.
   - [ ] b. a black hightop tennis shoe.
   - [ ] c. a naked woman lying by the side of the road.

3. Deputy Strasser found Christene Skubish's car after seeing
   - [ ] a. a child's hightop shoe on the road.
   - [ ] b. Nicky Skubish.
   - [ ] c. a naked woman by the side of the road.

4. Mysteriously, after five days, Christene Skubish's body
   - [ ] a. still smelled like the perfume she was wearing when she crashed.
   - [ ] b. had lost a lot of blood.
   - [ ] c. had not decayed at all.

5. The naked woman by the side of the road
   - [ ] a. was Christene Skubish.
   - [ ] b. remains a mystery.
   - [ ] c. was Nicky's guardian angel.

Score 5 points for each correct answer.

_____ **Total Score:** Recalling Facts

C | Making Inferences

When you combine your own experience with information from a text to draw a conclusion that is not directly stated in that text, you are making an inference. Below are five statements that may or may not be inferences based on information in the article. Label the statements using the following key:

C—Correct Inference   F—Faulty Inference

_____ 1. Christene Skubish meant to drive off the road.

_____ 2. Nicky didn't know how to dress himself.

_____ 3. Deborah Hoyt did not really see a naked body.

_____ 4. Deborah Hoyt often had hallucinations.

_____ 5. The black hightop shoe on the road belonged to Nicky Skubish.

Score 5 points for each correct answer.

_____ **Total Score:** Making Inferences

D | Using Words Precisely

Each numbered sentence below contains an underlined word or phrase from the article. Following the sentence are three definitions. One definition is closest to the meaning of the underlined word. One definition is opposite or nearly opposite. Label those two definitions using the following key; do not label the remaining definition.

C—Closest   O—Opposite or Nearly Opposite

1. The woman was curled up in a ball, with one arm thrown across her head as though <u>shielding</u> her face.

_____ a. covering

_____ b. showing

_____ c. touching

2. As he <u>crept</u> along, Strasser saw no sign of a woman anywhere.

_____ a. walked

_____ b. moved slowly

_____ c. sped

3. He couldn't believe Nicky had survived this long <u>amid</u> the wreckage.

_____ a. outside

_____ b. in

_____ c. after

4. In fact, Nicky Skubish was <u>on the verge of</u> death.

_____ a. far from

_____ b. looking for

_____ c. close to

5. "It's almost as though the condition of her body was <u>preserved</u> to make things easier for her son," mused Strasser.

_____ a. good

_____ b. kept from spoiling

_____ c. decayed

_____ Score 3 points for each correct C answer.

_____ Score 2 points for each correct O answer.

_____ **Total Score:** Using Words Precisely

Enter the four total scores in the spaces below, and add them together to find your Reading Comprehension Score. Then record your score on the graph on page 149.

Score	Question Type	Lesson 11
_____	Finding the Main Idea	
_____	Recalling Facts	
_____	Making Inferences	
_____	Using Words Precisely	
_____	**Reading Comprehension Score**	

Author's Approach

Put an X in the box next to the correct answer.

1. The main purpose of the first paragraph is to

☐ a. give the reader background information about the story.

☐ b. describe Christene Skubish.

☐ c. entertain the reader.

2. From the statements below, choose the one you believe the authors would agree with.

☐ a. Deborah Hoyt had seen Christene Skubish.

☐ b. The sheriff's department should continue investigating the Skubish case.

☐ c. Rich Strasser was a dedicated and compassionate deputy.

3. The authors tell this story mainly by

☐ a. retelling people's personal experiences.

☐ b. comparing people's accounts of the story.

☐ c. using their imagination.

_____ Number of correct answers

Record your personal assessment of your work on the Critical Thinking Chart on page 150.

Summarizing and Paraphrasing

Follow the directions provided for question 1. Put an X in the box next to the correct answer for questions 2 and 3.

1. Reread paragraph 3 in the article. Below, write a summary of the paragraph in no more than 25 words.

_____

_____

_____

Reread your summary and decide whether it covers the important ideas in the paragraph. Next, decide how to shorten the summary to 15 words or less without leaving out any essential information. Write this summary below.

_____

_____

_____

2. Below are summaries of the article. Choose the summary that says all the most important things about the article but in the fewest words.

☐ a. Nicky Skubish was saved after surviving five days in the wreckage of his mother's car because Deborah Hoyt saw a naked woman by the side of the road. Hoyt alerted the sheriff's department, who located Christene Skubish's car and found Nicky near death.

☐ b. The naked woman Deborah Hoyt saw along the side of the road alerted the sheriff's department to the location of Christene Skubish's car and saved her son Nicky's life.

☐ c. Nicky Skubish was near death when the sheriff's department located his mother's car five days after it had crashed.

3. Read the statement from the article below. Then read the paraphrase of that statement. Choose the reason that best tells why the paraphrase does not say the same thing as the statement.

Statement: "With his heart pumping wildly, Strasser slid down the steep bank."

Paraphrase: Strasser was very excited as he hurried down the steep bank.

☐ a. Paraphrase says too much.

☐ b. Paraphrase doesn't say enough.

☐ c. Paraphrase doesn't agree with the statement from the article.

_____ Number of correct answers

Record your personal assessment of your work on the Critical Thinking Chart on page 150.

Critical Thinking

Put an X in the box next to the correct answer for questions 1, 3, and 4. Follow the directions provided for question 2.

1. Which of the following statements from the article is an opinion rather than a fact?

   ☐ a. In the end, some people concluded the naked woman was an angel.

   ☐ b. When Strasser found Christene, she was still in the driver's seat of her car with the seatbelt fastened.

   ☐ c. Deputy Rich Strasser began to investigate but could find no leads.

2. Choose from the letters in the phrase bank below to correctly complete the following statement. Write the letters on the lines.

   Phrase bank:
   a. her son Nicky's life was saved
   b. find Christene Skubish's car
   c. the naked woman Deborah Hoyt saw

   According to the article, _____ caused Deputy Strasser to _____, and the effect was _____.

3. Based on the information in the article, you can predict that

   ☐ a. the sheriff's department will continue trying to solve the mysteries in the Skubish case.

   ☐ b. the mysteries in the Skubish case will never be solved.

   ☐ c. Nicky will go to live with his father.

4. Into which of the following theme categories would this story fit?

   ☐ a. science fiction

   ☐ b. mystery

   ☐ c. adventure

_____ Number of correct answers

Record your personal assessment of your work on the Critical Thinking Chart on page 150.

Personal Response

What was most surprising or interesting to you about this article?

_____

_____

_____

Self-Assessment

A word or phrase in the article that I do not understand is

_____

_____

_____

LESSON 12 A Shocking Experience

¹It could happen to you almost anywhere. You could be walking along the golf course. You could be enjoying an outdoor picnic or sailing on the open water. It could also happen as you talk on the phone, wash the dishes, or even as you watch TV. But the odds are very much against it. Only one person in about 600,000 ever gets struck by lightning.

2 Given those numbers, you'd have to call any lightning victim unlucky. But what do you call a person who has been hit *seven* times? incredibly unlucky? That hardly seems strong

Although the odds are against it, people can be struck by lightning just about anywhere.

enough. But you'd have to call Roy Sullivan something. Between 1942 and 1977, he was struck by lightning seven times. That is a world record.

3 Sullivan worked as a park ranger in Virginia. His first encounter with lightning cost him a big toe. Later hits scorched his eyebrows, singed his hair, and burned his shoulder. In 1973 Sullivan suffered the worst hit of his life. He was stepping out of his truck when lightning streaked toward him. "It set my hat and hair on fire," he later said. "Then it went down my left arm and leg, knocked off my shoe, and crossed over to my right leg. It also set my underwear on fire."

4 Despite Sullivan's record, Virginia is not the state with the most lightning. That distinction belongs to Florida. The peninsula of Florida lies between two warm bodies of water. High humidity and hot weather breed many violent storms. It is really bad during the hottest time of the year. That's when the "Sunshine State" gets bombarded with thunderstorms and lightning. About 5 million bolts of lightning strike Florida each year. That is far more than in any other state.

5 Lightning kills people every year. But it also does some strange things to people who get hit and somehow live. Take the case of Florida's George McBay. One day in 1993 he was helping to lower a large metal pipe from a roof. Suddenly, he was struck by lightning. "It felt like everything in my body just blew out the top of my head," he said.

6 The lightning bolt didn't kill McBay. But it changed his life forever. "The best day that I've had since the accident isn't as good as the worst day I had before the accident," McBay later said. "You get lost. Blackouts. A good day is lying on the couch."

7 Sherri Spain could sympathize with McBay. On August 27, 1989, Spain was in Maryville, Tennessee. She and her volleyball team were taking a lunch break outside a gym. As they ate, a storm rolled in. Spain really liked storms. She liked the crack of thunder and the flash of lightning. "My heart races during a storm," she once said.

8 So when the wind began to blow and the rain came, Spain stood just outside the gym with Dawn Platt, one of her students. All the other students

ran for cover back inside the gym. "It was stupid," she later admitted.

9   A lightning bolt hit the steel door directly behind Spain and entered the back of her head. She slumped to the ground. Platt knelt beside her, not knowing what to do. "I held her hand and called her name, but she didn't respond," Platt later recalled. "I thought she was dead. All I could do was scream for help and pray."

10   Spain lived, but the lightning affected her in many ways. She lost sight in her right eye and hearing in her right ear. Her hair, which had been dark brown, turned blonde. She developed heart trouble. Spain also lost much of her brain power. As a teacher, Spain had always valued her mental abilities. Yet suddenly she couldn't even remember the letters of the alphabet. It took her a year of grueling work to rebuild her basic skills. Even then she still had memory problems. She couldn't remember facts or dates. When she finally returned to the classroom, Spain spent hours each night preparing her lessons and had to use lots of notes.

11   It may seem hard to believe, but once in a great while being struck by lightning can be a blessing. In February 1971 Edwin Robinson lost control of his truck and crashed on an icy road in Maine. His head went through the back window. As a result, he suffered brain damage. Slowly, he lost his sight and much of his hearing. He had to learn Braille and wear a hearing aid. Robinson lived this way for nine years.

12   Then, on June 4, 1980, Robinson went for a short walk in the rain with his aluminum cane. Without warning, a bolt of lightning hit him and knocked him out. For 20 minutes, he lay unconscious on the ground. At last he woke up and returned to his house. He felt very tired, but otherwise he seemed fine. He decided to take a nap.

13   Then something remarkable happened. When he woke up from his nap, he could read the time on the kitchen clock. He hadn't been able to do that for nine years. Within a few days, he could see well enough to walk without a cane. His hearing also improved greatly. He even began to regrow some hair on his bald head.

14   Edwin Robinson's case is a rare exception. You don't want to test your luck by running around in a thunderstorm waving a golf club over your head. You should always treat lightning for what it is—a potential killer. Hurricanes and tornadoes make the news because they tend to kill in large numbers. Lightning picks off its victims one at a time. In the end, though, lightning kills more Americans than almost any other weather hazard.

15   The odds of getting struck by a bolt of lightning are still about as high as winning the lottery. But unlike the lottery, looking for lightning bolts is a game most people would rather not play.

If you have been timed while reading this article, enter your reading time below. Then turn to the Words-per-Minute Table on page 147 and look up your reading speed (words per minute). Enter your reading speed on the graph on page 148.

Reading Time: Lesson 12

_____ : _____

Minutes   Seconds

A Finding the Main Idea

One statement below expresses the main idea of the article. One statement is too general, or too broad. The other statement explains only part of the article; it is too narrow. Label the statements using the following key:

M—Main Idea   **B—Too Broad**   **N—Too Narrow**

_____ 1. The odds of being hit by lightning are very small.

_____ 2. Roy Sullivan was struck by lightning seven times in 35 years.

_____ 3. Lightning can have both good and bad effects on people who are struck by it and live.

_____ Score 15 points for a correct M answer.

_____ Score 5 points for each correct B or N answer.

_____ **Total Score:** Finding the Main Idea

B Recalling Facts

How well do you remember the facts in the article? Put an X in the box next to the answer that correctly completes each statement about the article.

1. When Roy Sullivan was struck by lightning in 1973,
   ☐ a. it scorched his eyebrows.
   ☐ b. it set his hat and hair on fire.
   ☐ c. he lost a big toe.

2. The state with the most lightning is
   ☐ a. Florida.
   ☐ b. Virginia.
   ☐ c. Tennessee.

3. After being hit by lightning, Sherri Spain
   ☐ a. lost sight in her left eye.
   ☐ b. could not return to teaching.
   ☐ c. had memory problems.

4. After Edwin Robinson was hit by lightning, he
   ☐ a. went for a short walk in the rain.
   ☐ b. needed a cane to walk.
   ☐ c. regained his sight and hearing.

5. Lightning
   ☐ a. kills people in large numbers.
   ☐ b. kills people one at a time.
   ☐ c. doesn't usually kill its victims.

Score 5 points for each correct answer.

_____ **Total Score:** Recalling Facts

C Making Inferences

When you combine your own experience with information from a text to draw a conclusion that is not directly stated in that text, you are making an inference. Below are five statements that may or may not be inferences based on information in the article. Label the statements using the following key:

C—Correct Inference   F—Faulty Inference

_____ 1. Most people who are hit by lightning are killed.

_____ 2. Lightning usually strikes people who are in a forest or a park.

_____ 3. Some people attract lightning more than others.

_____ 4. Lightning is drawn to metal objects.

_____ 5. When lightning hits someone, it usually affects the brain.

Score 5 points for each correct answer.

_____ **Total Score:** Making Inferences

D Using Words Precisely

Each numbered sentence below contains an underlined word or phrase from the article. Following the sentence are three definitions. One definition is closest to the meaning of the underlined word. One definition is opposite or nearly opposite. Label those two definitions using the following key; do not label the remaining definition.

C—Closest   O—Opposite or Nearly Opposite

1. High humidity and hot weather <u>breed</u> many violent storms.

_____ a. create

_____ b. stop

_____ c. combine

2. That's when the "Sunshine State" <u>gets bombarded with</u> thunderstorms and lightning.

_____ a. gets a lot of

_____ b. gets hit heavily by

_____ c. escapes

3. It took her a year of <u>grueling</u> work to rebuild her basic skills.

_____ a. easy

_____ b. mental

_____ c. difficult

4. Then something <u>remarkable</u> happened.

_____ a. amazing

_____ b. ordinary

_____ c. different

5. Lightning <u>picks off</u> its victims one at a time.

_____ a. kills

_____ b. helps

_____ c. chooses

_____ Score 3 points for each correct C answer.

_____ Score 2 points for each correct O answer.

_____ **Total Score:** Using Words Precisely

Enter the four total scores in the spaces below, and add them together to find your Reading Comprehension Score. Then record your score on the graph on page 149.

Then record your score on the graph on page 149.

Score	Question Type	Lesson 12
_____	Finding the Main Idea	
_____	Recalling Facts	
_____	Making Inferences	
_____	Using Words Precisely	
_____	**Reading Comprehension Score**	

Author's Approach

Put an X in the box next to the correct answer.

1. The authors use the first sentence of the article to

☐ a. entertain the reader.

☐ b. get the reader's attention.

☐ c. describe the qualities of lightning.

2. What is the authors' purpose in writing "A Shocking Experience?"

☐ a. to warn the reader about the danger of lightning strikes

☐ b. to express an opinion about lightning strikes

☐ c. to describe the effects of being hit by lightning

3. What do the authors imply by saying, "You don't want to test your luck by running around in a thunderstorm waving a golf club over your head"?

☐ a. You shouldn't play golf during a thunderstorm.

☐ b. Golf clubs attract lightning.

☐ c. Motion attracts lightning.

_____ Number of correct answers

Record your personal assessment of your work on the Critical Thinking Chart on page 150.

Record your personal assessment of your work on the Critical Thinking Chart on page 150.

CRITICAL THINKING

Summarizing and Paraphrasing

Follow the directions provided for questions 1 and 2. Put an X in the box next to the correct answer for question 3.

1. Look for the important ideas and events in paragraphs 5 and 6. Summarize those paragraphs in one or two sentences.

_____

_____

_____

2. Complete the following one-sentence summary of the article using the lettered phrases from the phrase bank below. Write the letters on the lines.

Phrase bank:

a. a warning about how dangerous lightning can be

b. figures about the odds of being hit by lightning

c. people who have been struck by lightning

The article about lightning begins with _____, goes on to

tell about _____, and ends with _____.

3. Choose the sentence that correctly restates the following sentence from the article: "High humidity and hot weather breed many violent storms."

☐ a. Many terrible storms are caused by the combination of high humidity and hot weather.

☐ b. In hot and humid weather there are more bad storms.

☐ c. Violent storms cause the weather to become hot and humid.

_____ Number of correct answers

Record your personal assessment of your work on the Critical Thinking Chart on page 150.

Critical Thinking

Put an X in the box next to the correct answer for questions 1 and 4. Follow the directions provided for the other questions.

1. Which of the following statements from the article is an opinion rather than a fact?

☐ a. Only one person in about 600,000 ever gets struck by lightning.

☐ b. Between 1942 and 1977, Roy Sullivan was struck by lightning seven times.

☐ c. "It felt like everything in my body just blew out the top of my head," he said.

2. Using what you know about lightning strikes and the information in the article, list ways in which Edwin Robinson's and Sherri Spain's experiences after being struck by lightning were similar and ways in which they were different.

Similarities

_____

_____

_____

Differences

_____

_____

_____

3. Choose from the letters below to correctly complete the following statement. Write the letters on the lines.

According to paragraphs 9 and 10, _____ because _____.

a. Sherri Spain was hit by lightning

b. the lightning affected her in many ways

c. she was standing near a steel door

4. What did you have to do to answer question 3?

☐ a. find a cause (why something happened)

☐ b. find a summary (synthesized information)

☐ c. find a purpose (why something is done)

_____ Number of correct answers

Record your personal assessment of your work on the Critical Thinking Chart on page 150.

Personal Response

A question I would like answered by Edwin Robinson is

_____

_____

_____

Self-Assessment

From reading this article, I have learned

_____

_____

_____

Crocker Land: An Arctic Mirage

[1]Robert Peary picked up his binoculars and looked toward the northwest. What he saw made his heart leap. On the far horizon he spotted a vast, snow-capped mountain range. It was something that didn't appear on any maps. "I looked longingly at this land," Peary wrote. He saw himself walking along its shores and climbing its mountains. But Peary wasn't prepared to do it on this trip.

Arctic mirages such as this are caused by a special mix of air that bends light.

2   The year was 1906. Robert Peary was on his way home. He had been exploring the polar area in far northern Canada. At the moment he was standing on Cape Thomas Hubbard at the tip of Axel Heiberg Land. He figured the land he saw was about 120 miles away. Peary built a cairn, or pile of rocks, to mark where he stood. Then he decided on a name for the faraway mountain range. He called it Crocker Land in honor of a man who had helped pay for this polar trip.

3   When Peary got back to America, he told people what he had seen. The image of Crocker Land fired people's imaginations. Some thought it might be a lost island continent. They thought it might hold great treasures of gold and iron ore. Others thought it would turn out to be unfrozen land filled with exciting new forms of life. They pictured it heated by under-ground "furnaces." People pointed out that Inuits talked of a distant land warmed by the sun and filled with herds of animals. Said one man, "If

there be an ice-cooled desert, why not a steam-heated polar paradise?"

4   But where exactly was this unmapped land? The American Museum of Natural History decided to find out. In 1913 it sent an expedition to find Crocker Land. The search was led by Donald MacMillan, who had been a member of Peary's last polar expedition. Fitzhugh Green was second in command. That July they headed north. They ran into trouble all along the way. Some of their sled dogs died. The snow was so loose they could not build good igloos. Several Inuits who joined them got sick with mumps and flu. Winter temperatures dropped as low as 50 degrees below zero. Trying to keep warm one night, MacMillan set fire to his sleeping bag by mistake. "I was warm at last," he joked in his journal.

5   On April 13, 1914, they finally reached Cape Thomas Hubbard. At least, they thought it was the cape. MacMillan and Green searched for the cairn Peary had left eight years before. They couldn't find it. They looked

through their binoculars, hoping to get their first glimpse of Crocker Land. They saw nothing but an endless sea of white. Undaunted, they decided to head northwest across the frozen sea anyway. They planned to keep going until they reached Crocker Land.

6   A little way out they looked back and saw they had missed the cape by a few miles. That didn't matter. MacMillan and Green knew where they were, and they knew Crocker Land was just 120 miles away.

7   As they continued, the expedition again ran into difficulties. The biggest problem was leads, or stretches of open water. These leads were impossible to cross. Usually, a good cold night would do the trick. Still, it was dangerous to cross freshly frozen water. At one point several sled dogs broke through the new ice. Luckily, they were pulled out before shifting chunks of ice could crush them.

8   At last, on the morning of April 21, Green shouted to MacMillan, who was still in his igloo. Green said he could see Crocker Land. MacMillan climbed

to the peak of a nearby iceberg. "Sure enough!" he wrote in his journal. "There it was as plain as day—hills, valleys, and ice cap, a tremendous land stretching . . . [across] the horizon."

9   But as the group moved closer to Crocker Land, a strange thing happened. The land seemed to move away from them. When they stopped, the land stopped. When they moved again, the land receded again. Also, the distant land seemed to change shape. MacMillan wrote, "As we watched it more narrowly its appearance slowly changed."

10   As evening approached Crocker Land faded from view. The next day, they marched toward it again. "On this day there was the same appearance of land in the west," wrote MacMillan. "But it gradually faded away towards evening."

11   By April 23 the Inuits were growing restless. They began to drop hints about going home. Some scoffed that Crocker Land was nothing but mist in the sky. MacMillan did not want to hear this. He took out his map and showed it to them. The map had a brown spot where Crocker Land was supposed to be. MacMillan said he was not going to turn back until he reached it.

12   So the group pushed ahead. Green, however, stayed behind to take some measurements. Later that day, Green caught up with MacMillan. He showed him what he had learned. They were now 150 miles due northwest from Cape Thomas Hubbard. Yet Peary had said that Crocker Land was only 120 miles from the cape.

13   The news hit MacMillan hard. He suddenly realized that there must not be a Crocker Land after all. He later wrote, "We had not only reached the brown spot on the map, but were 30 miles [past it]. We scanned every foot of that horizon. [There was] nothing in sight." There were no valleys, no mountains, no land at all. There was nothing but a vast sheet of ice in all directions.

14   The expedition had been chasing a mirage. The valleys and mountains they "saw" were just a trick played on them by the forces of nature. Such illusions are caused by a special mix of air that bends light. It was like seeing a pool of water on a dry road. In the Arctic, these illusions can appear on a grand scale. An iceberg can look like a city.

15   Crestfallen, the explorers turned toward home. On April 28 they reached Cape Thomas Hubbard. This time MacMillan and Green found the cairn left by Peary. That meant they were standing on the very spot where Peary first saw Crocker Land. The two men looked out at the horizon. And what did they see? "There was land everywhere," wrote Donald MacMillan. "Had we not just come from far over the horizon, we would have returned to our country and reported land as Peary did."

16   A few years later planes flew over the whole area. They proved beyond all doubt that no Crocker Land existed. The top of the world hid no lost continent, no heated paradise. There was just ice, ice, and more ice.

A | Finding the Main Idea

One statement below expresses the main idea of the article. One statement is too general, or too broad. The other statement explains only part of the article; it is too narrow. Label the statements using the following key:

M—Main Idea   **B—Too Broad**   **N—Too Narrow**

_____ 1. In the Arctic, there are often large mirages that can look like land.

_____ 2. After spending time and money searching for Crocker Land, Donald MacMillan's team discovered that it was only a mirage.

_____ 3. As MacMillan's group moved toward Crocker Land, the land moved further away from them.

_____ Score 15 points for a correct M answer.

_____ Score 5 points for each correct B or N answer.

_____ **Total Score:** Finding the Main Idea

B | Recalling Facts

How well do you remember the facts in the article? Put an X in the box next to the answer that correctly completes each statement about the article.

1. In 1906 Robert Peary thought he saw
   - ☐ a. a steam-heated polar paradise.
   - ☐ b. an unmapped stretch of land.
   - ☐ c. Cape Thomas Hubbard.

2. In 1913 the American Museum of Natural History
   - ☐ a. sent Robert Peary to find Crocker Land.
   - ☐ b. discovered the location of Crocker Land.
   - ☐ c. sent an expedition to find Crocker Land.

3. MacMillan's expedition had difficulty
   - ☐ a. crossing leads, or open stretches of water.
   - ☐ b. walking across shifting chunks of ice.
   - ☐ c. following the map.

4. As the men moved closer to Crocker Land,
   - ☐ a. they could see it more clearly.
   - ☐ b. it looked more narrow.
   - ☐ c. it seemed to move away from them.

5. MacMillan realized there was no Crocker Land when
   - ☐ a. the Inuits told him it was only mist in the sky.
   - ☐ b. he had passed the point where Crocker Land should have been.
   - ☐ c. he could no longer see Crocker Land.

Score 5 points for each correct answer.

_____ **Total Score:** Recalling Facts

C | Making Inferences

When you combine your own experience with information from a text to draw a conclusion that is not directly stated in that text, you are making an inference. Below are five statements that may or may not be inferences based on information in the article. Label the statements using the following key:

C—Correct Inference   F—Faulty Inference

_____ 1. People were interested in the idea of an unexplored piece of land.

_____ 2. Peary did not have enough money to search for Crocker Land in 1906.

_____ 3. People believed Peary when he reported seeing land beyond Cape Thomas Hubbard.

_____ 4. MacMillan's expedition traveled on foot.

_____ 5. The Inuits knew that Crocker Land was a mirage before MacMillan did.

Score 5 points for each correct answer.

_____ **Total Score:** Making Inferences

D | Using Words Precisely

Each numbered sentence below contains an underlined word or phrase from the article. Following the sentence are three definitions. One definition is closest to the meaning of the underlined word. One definition is opposite or nearly opposite. Label those two definitions using the following key; do not label the remaining definition.

C—Closest   O—Opposite or Nearly Opposite

1. <u>Undaunted</u>, they decided to head northwest across the frozen sea anyway.

_____ a. discouraged

_____ b. determined

_____ c. confused

2. MacMillan climbed to the <u>peak</u> of a nearby iceberg.

_____ a. edge

_____ b. base

_____ c. tip

3. When the men moved again, the land <u>receded</u> again.

_____ a. moved away

_____ b. moved closer

_____ c. disappeared

4. There was nothing but a <u>vast</u> sheet of ice in all directions.

_____ a. thick

_____ b. huge

_____ c. tiny

5. <u>Crestfallen</u>, the explorers turned toward home.

_____ a. discouraged

_____ b. hopeful

_____ c. happy

_____ Score 3 points for each correct C answer.

_____ Score 2 points for each correct O answer.

_____ **Total Score:** Using Words Precisely

Enter the four total scores in the spaces below, and add them together to find your Reading Comprehension Score. Then record your score on the graph on page 149.

Score	Question Type	Lesson 13
_____	Finding the Main Idea	
_____	Recalling Facts	
_____	Making Inferences	
_____	Using Words Precisely	
_____	**Reading Comprehension Score**	

Author's Approach

Put an X in the box next to the correct answer.

1. The main purpose of the first paragraph is to

☐ a. introduce the topic of the article.

☐ b. introduce the character of Robert Peary.

☐ c. describe Crocker Land.

2. What do the authors mean by the statement, "The image of Crocker Land fired people's imaginations"?

☐ a. People were very interested in Peary's description of Crocker Land.

☐ b. People were intrigued by the idea of a new, unexplored land.

☐ c. People had different ideas about what Crocker Land looked like.

3. Which of the following statements from the article best describes Donald MacMillan's feelings after he discovered that Crocker Land did not exist?

☐ a. He suddenly realized that there was no 'Crocker Land' after all.

☐ b. The men had been chasing a mirage.

☐ c. Crestfallen, the explorers turned toward home.

_____ Number of correct answers

Record your personal assessment of your work on the Critical Thinking Chart on page 150.

Summarizing and Paraphrasing

Follow the directions provided for questions 1 and 2. Put an X in the box next to the correct answer for question 3.

1. Reread paragraphs 8 and 9 in the article. Below, write a summary of the paragraphs in no more than 25 words.

_____

_____

_____

Reread your summary and decide whether it covers the important ideas in the paragraph. Next, decide how to shorten the summary to 15 words or less without leaving out any essential information. Write this summary below.

_____

_____

_____

2. Look for the important ideas and events in paragraphs 11 and 12. Summarize those paragraphs in one or two sentences.

_____

_____

_____

3. Choose the best one-sentence paraphrase for the following sentence from the article: "Some scoffed that Crocker Land was nothing but mist in the sky."

☐ a. Some said that Crocker Land didn't really exist.

☐ b. Some said that they would never reach Crocker Land.

☐ c. Some joked that Crocker Land was really a land in the sky.

_____ Number of correct answers

Record your personal assessment of your work on the Critical Thinking Chart on page 150.

Critical Thinking

Put an X in the box next to the correct answer for questions 1 and 3. Follow the directions provided for questions 2 and 4.

1. For each statement below, write O if it expresses an opinion or F if it expresses a fact.

_____ a. They thought it might hold great treasures of gold and iron ore.

_____ b. As they continued, the men again ran into difficulties.

_____ c. Some scoffed that Crocker Land was nothing but mist in the sky.

2. What was the effect of Green's taking measurements to figure out the expedition's position?

☐ a. They realized they had missed Crocker Land.

☐ b. They realized that they had been going in the wrong direction.

☐ c. They realized that there was no Crocker Land.

3. In which paragraphs did you find the information you needed to answer question 2?

_____

4. Based on the information in the article, you can predict that

☐ a. MacMillan did not go on any more Arctic expeditions after the Crocker Land expedition.

☐ b. Robert Peary was disappointed by the results of MacMillan's expedition.

☐ c. People were not interested in new lands anymore after hearing about Crocker Land.

_____ Number of correct answers

Record your personal assessment of your work on the Critical Thinking Chart on page 150.

Personal Response

I know how Donald MacMillan felt when he realized there was no Crocker Land because

_____

_____

_____

_____

Self-Assessment

Before reading this article, I already knew

_____

_____

_____

_____

Fish Killer

1 "I was disoriented," said Dr. JoAnn Burkholder, a scientist at North Carolina State University. "I had burning eyes. I couldn't remember how to dial a telephone number. I couldn't write. It was all very frightening."

2 Burkholder knew what was causing these strange symptoms. After all, she was the one who first discovered the culprit.

3 Her problems were caused by a bizarre member of the algae family. It is a microbe so small it has just one cell. Burkholder named it *Pfiesteria piscicida*. That is Latin for "fish killer."

When Pfiesteria attacks, millions of dead fish wash ashore. Sometimes there are so many that bulldozers are needed to remove them.

4 Burkholder first came across this microbe in 1989. A fellow scientist was having trouble with some laboratory fish. The fish kept dying. Burkholder took a careful look at them. She discovered that they were being attacked by the Pfiesteria microbe.

5 Two years later Burkholder was running more tests on the microbe. She did not think she was doing anything dangerous. But it turned out Pfiesteria could give off deadly fumes. Burkholder breathed in those fumes. That's when she grew sick and confused. Her research aide also grew ill. He had to crawl out of the lab on his hands and knees. It took him months to recover.

6 The lab wasn't the only place the microbe was causing trouble. In 1991, huge numbers of fish suddenly began dying in North Carolina's Pamlico Sound. Burkholder suspected Pfiesteria was to blame. She was right. The microbe was poisoning, then eating, the fish. Since then there have been other fish kills in the state. There have also been fish kills in Virginia and Maryland.

7 How could such a tiny creature do so much damage? In fact, most of the time the microbe doesn't do any damage at all. It lives in small numbers in the mud at the mouths of rivers. Mostly it feeds on bacteria and other algae and stays out of trouble. That's why no one even knew it was a threat until 1991.

8 But under just the right conditions, the microbe earns its nickname of "the cell from hell." It multiplies or "blooms" very fast. It swells in size. It begins to show both plant and animal features. Amazingly, the microbe can change into 24 different shapes. No other known creature can do that. It changes shape depending on what it plans to eat.

9 When fish is on the menu, Pfiesteria grows two little tails. It uses these to swim toward its prey. Drawing near, it shoots a deadly poison or toxin into the water. This toxin stuns all fish in the area. The fish become dazed and confused. They begin to gasp for oxygen. They start swimming upside down or in circles. As they die, the microbe moves in to eat their flesh.

10   Pfiesteria often goes years without causing any harm. When the microbe does bloom, it is usually between April and October. Also, the blooms only occur in certain spots. The microbe is not found in the open ocean or in rivers far from the coast. It only lives where the fresh water of a river meets the salt water of the sea. In these spots the water moves slowly. That makes it the perfect home for Pfiesteria.

11   Most importantly, perhaps, the microbe only blooms when there are a lot of fish around. It may be that the fish themselves give off some chemical that wakes up the Pfiesteria. Or perhaps water pollution does the trick. Fertilizers or animal waste from nearby farms could be to blame. These substances often attract large numbers of fish. But they might also cause the Pfiesteria to bloom.

12   While no one really knows what causes the microbe to attack, scientists agree that the results are gruesome. Fishermen are often the first to spot an attack. They begin to see fish with red open sores all over their bodies. A short while later, millions of dead fish wash ashore. Workers need bulldozers to get rid of all the dead bodies. Seeing such a fish kill is not fun. River officials in North Carolina know how bad it can be. "We had some folks on the boat with us [who] were seeing [a fish kill] for the first time," said one. "These were grown men. They were actually crying."

13   Then there is the danger to humans. After all, fumes from the microbe made Dr. Burkholder and her aide sick. Couldn't they do the same to other people? "I think Pfiesteria should be taken very seriously," Burkholder said in 1997. She believes the microbe could be a serious health problem.

14   Others disagree. North Carolina's health director is not convinced that Pfiesteria is a threat to humans. Still, he has praised Burkholder's work and called her "an outstanding scientist." He knows that people have many questions about Pfiesteria. "We want to know the answers," he said.

15   Some things are already known. The microbe is not going to cause the next plague. Scientists say that it can't be "caught" like a cold or flu. Still, it can be dangerous for anyone who is around when the toxin is shot out. It is not wise to be in the water at such a time. Scientists say that breathing the fumes from the toxin can also be harmful. As Dr. Burkholder found, that can cause headaches, skin rashes, muscle cramps, and loss of memory.

16   Some people, though, can't avoid the fumes. Shipbuilders and fishermen are around the water all the time. In North Carolina, about 100 of these people seem to have been affected by Pfiesteria blooms. One shipbuilder said, "I had sores . . . for over a month, stomach cramping, and shaking."

17   The state of North Carolina is taking the threat to humans seriously. State officials keep watch on rivers and bays. If there is a fish kill, they post warning signs urging people not to swim, fish, or boat on the water. Sometimes the state just shuts down certain waterways. People are not allowed on them until the danger has passed. So even if "the cell from hell" hasn't killed anyone yet, it has caused a lot of waves.

If you have been timed while reading this article, enter your reading time below. Then turn to the Words-per-Minute Table on page 147 and look up your reading speed (words per minute). Enter your reading speed on the graph on page 148.

Reading Time: Lesson 14

_____ : _____
Minutes   *Seconds*

A | Finding the Main Idea

One statement below expresses the main idea of the article. One statement is too general, or too broad. The other statement explains only part of the article; it is too narrow. Label the statements using the following key:

M—Main Idea   **B—Too Broad**   **N—Too Narrow**

_____ 1. Pfiesteria piscicida is a simple organism that can cause a lot of problems.

_____ 2. A single-celled microbe named Pfiesteria piscicida can kill fish and be a danger to humans under certain conditions.

_____ 3. Pfiesteria piscicida only causes problems when it blooms.

_____ Score 15 points for a correct M answer.

_____ Score 5 points for each correct B or N answer.

_____ **Total Score:** Finding the Main Idea

B | Recalling Facts

How well do you remember the facts in the article? Put an X in the box next to the answer that correctly completes each statement about the article.

1. Dr. JoAnn Burkholder discovered Pfiesteria piscicida
   ☐ a. when she grew sick and confused.
   ☐ b. after witnessing a fish kill in North Carolina's Pamlico Sound.
   ☐ c. when she was studying dying laboratory fish.

2. Pfiesteria piscicida
   ☐ a. usually feeds on large fish.
   ☐ b. is usually harmless.
   ☐ c. lives in the open ocean.

3. When Pfiesteria multiplies, or blooms, it
   ☐ a. changes shape.
   ☐ b. shoots a deadly poison into its prey.
   ☐ c. doesn't cause any damage at all.

4. Pfiesteria blooms occur only
   ☐ a. in salt water.
   ☐ b. when there are a lot of fish around.
   ☐ c. in the spring.

5. Scientists have learned that
   ☐ a. Pfiesteria is not dangerous to humans.
   ☐ b. fertilizers and animal waste "wake up" Pfiesteria.
   ☐ c. Pfiesteria can't be "caught" like a cold.

Score 5 points for each correct answer.

_____ **Total Score:** Recalling Facts

C Making Inferences

When you combine your own experience with information from a text to draw a conclusion that is not directly stated in that text, you are making an inference. Below are five statements that may or may not be inferences based on information in the article. Label the statements using the following key:

C—Correct Inference   F—Faulty Inference

_____ 1. No fish were killed by Pfiesteria before 1989.

_____ 2. Pfiesteria is not contagious.

_____ 3. Pfiesteria does not cause permanent damage to humans.

_____ 4. Pfiesteria thrives in warmer climates.

_____ 5. Scientists can predict when Pfiesteria will attack.

Score 5 points for each correct answer.

_____ **Total Score:** Making Inferences

D Using Words Precisely

Each numbered sentence below contains an underlined word or phrase from the article. Following the sentence are three definitions. One definition is closest to the meaning of the underlined word. One definition is opposite or nearly opposite. Label those two definitions using the following key; do not label the remaining definition.

C—Closest   O—Opposite or Nearly Opposite

1. "I was <u>disoriented</u>," said Dr. JoAnn Burkholder, a scientist at North Carolina State University.

_____ a. confused

_____ b. focused

_____ c. ill

2. Burkholder <u>suspected</u> Pfiesteria was to blame.

_____ a. doubted

_____ b. believed

_____ c. proved

3. It <u>swells</u> in size.

_____ a. shrinks

_____ b. changes

_____ c. grows

4. North Carolina's health director is not convinced that Pfiesteria is <u>a threat</u> to humans.

_____ a. a danger

_____ b. helpful

_____ c. a worry

5. If there is a fish kill, they <u>post</u> warning signs.

_____ a. remove

_____ b. mail

_____ c. put up

_____ Score 3 points for each correct C answer.

_____ Score 2 points for each correct O answer.

_____ **Total Score:** Using Words Precisely

Enter the four total scores in the spaces below, and add them together to find your Reading Comprehension Score. Then record your score on the graph on page 149.

Score	Question Type	Lesson 14
_____	Finding the Main Idea	
_____	Recalling Facts	
_____	Making Inferences	
_____	Using Words Precisely	
_____	**Reading Comprehension Score**	

Author's Approach

Put an X in the box next to the correct answer.

1. What is the authors' purpose in writing "Fish Killer?"

☐ a. to entertain the reader

☐ b. to inform the reader about Pfiesteria piscicida

☐ c. to express an opinion about Pfiesteria piscicida

2. Which of the following statements from the article best describes the effects of Pfiesteria piscicida on humans?

☐ a. Her research aide also grew ill. He had to crawl out of the lab on his hands and knees.

☐ b. "I was disoriented," said Dr. JoAnn Burkholder.

☐ c. Scientists say that breathing fumes from the toxin . . . can cause headaches, skin rashes, muscle cramps, and loss of memory.

3. The main purpose of the first paragraph is to

☐ a. get the reader's attention.

☐ b. describe the effects of Pfiesteria piscicida.

☐ c. introduce Dr. JoAnn Burkholder.

_____ Number of correct answers

Record your personal assessment of your work on the Critical Thinking Chart on page 150.

Summarizing and Paraphrasing

Follow the directions provided for each question.

1. Look for the important ideas and events in paragraphs 10 and 11. Summarize those paragraphs in one or two sentences.

_____

_____

_____

2. Complete the following one-sentence summary of the article using the lettered phrases from the phrase bank below. Write the letters on the lines.

> **Phrase bank:**
> a. an explanation of what is being done about it
> b. a description of the effects it has had on some scientists
> c. what it is and how it can affect fish

The article about Pfiesteria piscicida begins with _____,

goes on to explain _____, and ends with _____.

3. Read the statement from the article below. Then read the paraphrase of that statement. Choose the reason that best tells why the paraphrase does not say the same thing as the statement.

Statement: "It multiplies or 'blooms' very fast."

Paraphrase: It grows rapidly and develops new features.

☐ a. Paraphrase says too much.

☐ b. Paraphrase doesn't say enough.

☐ c. Paraphrase doesn't agree with the statement from the article.

> _____ Number of correct answers
>
> Record your personal assessment of your work on the Critical Thinking Chart on page 150.

Critical Thinking

Put an X in the box next to the correct answer for questions 1 and 2. Follow the directions provided for questions 3 and 4.

1. Which of the following statements from the article is an opinion rather than a fact?

☐ a. North Carolina's health director is not convinced that Pfiesteria is a threat to humans.

☐ b. Pfiesteria often goes years without causing any harm.

☐ c. Amazingly, the microbe can change into 24 different shapes.

2. From the information in the article, you can predict that

☐ a. Pfiesteria will spread to more states.

☐ b. there will not be a Pfiesteria outbreak for many years.

☐ c. scientists will continue to study Pfiesteria and its effects.

3. Which paragraphs provide evidence from the article to support your answer to question 2?

_____

4. Choose from the letters below to correctly complete the following statement. Write the letters on the lines.

According to paragraph 15, _____ can cause _____.

a. breathing fumes from the Pfiesteria toxin

b. be harmful to humans

c. headaches, muscle cramps, and other health problems

_____ Number of correct answers

Record your personal assessment of your work on the Critical Thinking Chart on page 150.

Personal Response

I wonder why

_____

_____

_____

_____

Self-Assessment

What concepts or ideas from the article were difficult? Which ones were easy?

_____

_____

_____

_____

The Case of the Missing Pilot

[1]"Is there any known traffic below five thousand [feet]?" asked Frederick Valentich, a 20-year-old pilot.

[2] "No known traffic," answered air traffic control official Steve Robey.

[3] It was October 21, 1978. Valentich was flying a single-engine Cessna plane from Melbourne, Australia, to King Island. He had taken off shortly before 6:30 P.M. His flight plan called for him to fly over Bass Strait. It was

On the night Frederick Valentich disappeared, Steve Robey was tracking air traffic on a monitor like this one. The object that Valentich described did not appear on Robey's monitor.

not supposed to be a long flight. It should have taken less than 70 minutes.

4   But at 7:06 P.M., Valentich saw something outside his cockpit window. He radioed the control tower to find out if there were any other planes in the area.

5   Valentich told Robey he saw what looked like "a large aircraft below five thousand [feet]."

6   "What type of aircraft is it?" asked Robey.

7   "I cannot affirm," Valentich radioed. He noted that it had four bright lights that looked like landing lights. Then he added, "The aircraft has just passed over me at least a thousand feet above." He said it was traveling too fast for him to tell how big it was.

8   As Valentich and Robey talked, Valentich again asked if there were any planes in the air near him. Again Robey assured him that there were "no known aircraft."

9   But whatever it was, it was still visible out Valentich's window. "It's approaching now from due east towards me," Valentich said. "It seems to me that [the pilot is] playing some sort of game. He's flying over me two

or three times at speeds I could not identify."

10   "What is your actual level?" asked Robey.

11   "My level is four and a half thousand [feet]. Four five zero zero."

12   Then Valentich radioed another message—one that stunned Steve Robey. "It's not an aircraft," Valentich said.

13   Robey asked him to describe whatever it was. But the object was still moving too fast for Valentich to get a good look.

14   "It's a long shape," Valentich radioed. "Cannot identify more than [that because] it has such speed. It's before me right now."

15   "How large would the—er—object be?" asked Robey.

16   Valentich did not respond to that question. He was too focused on what was happening outside his window. As he watched, the object suddenly appeared to stop moving. "It seems like it's stationary," Valentich announced. "What I'm doing right now is orbiting, and the thing is just orbiting on top of me. Also, it's got a green light and [is] sort of metallic. It's all shiny on the outside."

17   The incident was becoming more and more bizarre. After a few seconds, Valentich reported that the object had vanished. Then it came back, this time flying at him from the southwest.

18   Just at that moment Valentich began to have trouble with his plane. "The engine is rough idling," he reported. "I've got it set at twenty three twenty four, and the thing is coughing."

19   Robey asked Valentich what he planned to do.

20   "My intentions are—ah—to go to King Island," he answered. "That strange aircraft is hovering on top of me again. It is hovering, and it's not an aircraft."

21   For the next 17 seconds Valentich's microphone remained on. But he didn't say anything more. All Robey heard was a metallic scraping sound. After that, there was nothing but silence. That was the last anyone ever heard from Frederick Valentich.

22   When Valentich failed to show up on King Island, Australian officials started to look for him and his plane. The sky was clear and the winds were light, so weather did not hamper the

search. It would not have been a factor in Valentich's disappearance either. For four days searchers scoured the Bass Strait. They found nothing. The plane had a radio beacon that was supposed to give out a signal in case of trouble. But no signal was ever sent.

23   Searchers did find an oil slick about 18 miles north of King Island. Could this have been where Valentich's plane had crashed into Bass Strait? Tests showed that the oil was not aviation fuel. So the slick couldn't have been from the plane. So what happened to the pilot and the plane? After all these years, that's still an unanswered question. Some people believe that an unidentified flying object—a UFO—was somehow involved. Paul Norman of the Victorian UFO Research Society thinks so. Said Norman, "There is no doubt in my mind that the disappearance of Frederick Valentich and his Cessna was caused by a UFO."

24   Norman pointed out that other people saw strange things in the sky over Bass Strait that same day. About 2 P.M., a woman saw an odd object moving west across the sky. It stopped and hovered for a few minutes. Then it took off again, this time heading east.

25   Two hours later, another woman and her son saw two cigar-shaped objects move silently through the sky. The objects were silver at first, and then became white. Right after that they turned sharply and shot off.

26   More sightings came between 7:00 and 8:00 P.M. That was right around the time Valentich disappeared. Some people saw a glowing object that seemed to change from red to pink to white. Others saw something that was shaped like a starfish and gave off a low pulsating hum. Yet another eyewitness saw an object that did "impossible acrobatics" for five minutes and then flew off.

27   One group of witnesses even saw what may have been Valentich's plane with a UFO hovering above it. A man was hunting rabbits with his son and two nieces near Bass Strait. One of the girls looked up and saw a green light in the sky. "What is that light?" she asked.

28   "An airplane light," answered her uncle. "No," said the niece, "The light above the airplane."

29   The uncle didn't have an answer to her question.

30   No one else had any answers either. In 1982, the government of Australia issued its official report. It said the exact spot where the plane disappeared was not known. The exact time was not known either. In fact, the whole thing was a mystery. In the words of the report, "The reason for the disappearance of the aircraft has not been determined."

31   The report assumed that whatever had happened, Valentich had died. But no one knows that for sure. Perhaps Valentich faked his own death. Perhaps he became disoriented and flew in the wrong direction, crashing where search parties did not look. Perhaps he was even abducted by the object he saw. In the end, all we really know is that Frederick Valentich and his plane disappeared into thin air on October 21, 1978. It doesn't seem likely that we will ever know more than that.

If you have been timed while reading this article, enter your reading time below. Then turn to the Words-per-Minute Table on page 147 and look up your reading speed (words per minute). Enter your reading speed on the graph on page 148.

Reading Time: Lesson 15

_____ : _____
Minutes   Seconds

A | Finding the Main Idea

One statement below expresses the main idea of the article. One statement is too general, or too broad. The other statement explains only part of the article; it is too narrow. Label the statements using the following key:

M—Main Idea   B—Too Broad   N—Too Narrow

_____   1. No one knows what happened to Frederick Valentich on October 21, 1978.

_____   2. Pilot Frederick Valentich disappeared mysteriously after reporting a strange object flying near his plane.

_____   3. Pilot Frederick Valentich reported seeing a long, metallic object with a green light flying near him.

_____   Score 15 points for a correct M answer.

_____   Score 5 points for each correct B or N answer.

_____   **Total Score:** Finding the Main Idea

B | Recalling Facts

How well do you remember the facts in the article? Put an X in the box next to the answer that correctly completes each statement about the article.

1. Frederick Valentich radioed the control tower to
   ☐ a. report seeing a UFO.
   ☐ b. find out if there were any other planes in the area.
   ☐ c. check his flight plan.

2. Valentich reported that the object
   ☐ a. had four blue lights.
   ☐ b. was flying at 4,500 feet.
   ☐ c. was moving too fast for him to tell how big it was.

3. The last thing Robey heard from Valentich was
   ☐ a. the phrase, "It is hovering, and it's not an aircraft."
   ☐ b. the sound of Valentich's plane coughing.
   ☐ c. a metallic scraping sound.

4. Searchers looking for Valentich
   ☐ a. found no trace of either the pilot or his plane.
   ☐ b. saw strange objects in the sky.
   ☐ c. concluded that a UFO caused Valentich's disappearance.

5. On the evening of Valentich's disappearance,
   ☐ a. a man reported seeing Valentich's plane in the sky.
   ☐ b. several people saw strange, glowing objects in the sky.
   ☐ c. he faked his death.

Score 5 points for each correct answer.

_____   **Total Score:** Recalling Facts

C Making Inferences

When you combine your own experience with information from a text to draw a conclusion that is not directly stated in that text, you are making an inference. Below are five statements that may or may not be inferences based on information in the article. Label the statements using the following key:

C—Correct Inference   F—Faulty Inference

_____ 1. Frederick Valentich believed in UFOs.

_____ 2. Frederick Valentich was not a very good pilot.

_____ 3. The strange objects people reported seeing on the day of Valentich's disappearance were UFOs.

_____ 4. Valentich was curious about the object flying near him.

_____ 5. The Australian government knows what happened to Valentich.

Score 5 points for each correct answer.

_____ **Total Score:** Making Inferences

D Using Words Precisely

Each numbered sentence below contains an underlined word or phrase from the article. Following the sentence are three definitions. One definition is closest to the meaning of the underlined word. One definition is opposite or nearly opposite. Label those two definitions using the following key; do not label the remaining definition.

C—Closest   O—Opposite or Nearly Opposite

1. "I cannot <u>affirm</u>," Valentich radioed.

_____ a. deny

_____ b. say for sure

_____ c. report

2. Then Valentich radioed another message—one that <u>stunned</u> Steve Robey.

_____ a. stopped

_____ b. shocked

_____ c. didn't surprise

3. "It seems like it's <u>stationary</u>," Valentich announced.

_____ a. still

_____ b. long

_____ c. moving

4. For four days, searchers <u>scoured</u> Bass Strait.

_____ a. studied

_____ b. skimmed

_____ c. searched thoroughly

5. Perhaps he was even <u>abducted</u> by the UFO he saw.

_____ a. kidnapped

_____ b. returned

_____ c. killed

_____ Score 3 points for each correct C answer.

_____ Score 2 points for each correct O answer.

_____ **Total Score:** Using Words Precisely

Enter the four total scores in the spaces below, and add them together to find your Reading Comprehension Score. Then record your score on the graph on page 149.

Score	Question Type	Lesson 15
_____	Finding the Main Idea	
_____	Recalling Facts	
_____	Making Inferences	
_____	Using Words Precisely	
_____	**Reading Comprehension Score**	

Author's Approach

Put an X in the box next to the correct answer.

1. What is the authors' purpose in writing "The Case of the Missing Pilot"?

☐ a. to express an opinion about Frederick Valentich's disappearance

☐ b. to entertain the reader

☐ c. to inform the reader about Frederick Valentich's disappearance

2. The authors tell this story mainly by

☐ a. retelling people's personal experiences.

☐ b. comparing Frederick Valentich's disappearance with other similar stories.

☐ c. presenting Frederick Valentich's point of view.

3. Which of the following statements from the article best describes the object Valentich saw?

☐ a. "It's a long shape."

☐ b. "It's got a green light and [is] sort of metallic. It's all shiny on the outside."

☐ c. "That strange aircraft is hovering on top of me again. It is hovering, and it's not an aircraft."

_____ Number of correct answers

Record your personal assessment of your work on the Critical Thinking Chart on page 150.

Summarizing and Paraphrasing

Follow the directions provided for question 1. Put an X in the box next to the correct answer for questions 2 and 3.

1. Look for the important ideas and events in paragraph 16. Summarize the paragraph in one or two sentences.

_____

_____

_____

2. Below are summaries of the article. Choose the summary that says all the most important things about the article but in the fewest words.

☐ a. Frederick Valentich disappeared after reporting a strange object flying near him.

☐ b. Air traffic controller Steve Robey lost contact with Frederick Valentich after Valentich reported a strange object flying near him. Others on the ground also reported seeing similar objects. No trace of Valentich was ever found.

☐ c. Pilot Frederick Valentich disappeared without a trace after reporting a strange object flying near him. Other people in the area also reported seeing similar objects in the sky.

3. Choose the best one-sentence paraphrase for the following sentence from the article: "His flight plan called for him to fly over Bass Strait."

☐ a. He had decided to fly over Bass Strait.

☐ b. He had been instructed to fly over Bass Strait.

☐ c. He planned to fly straight to King Island.

_____ Number of correct answers

Record your personal assessment of your work on the Critical Thinking Chart on page 150.

Critical Thinking

Follow the directions provided for questions 1 and 2. Put an X in the box next to the correct answer for questions 3 and 4.

1. For each statement below, write O if it expresses an opinion or F if it expresses a fact.

_____ a. But at 7:06 P.M., Valentich saw something out his cockpit window.

_____ b. "It seems to me that he's playing some sort of game."

_____ c. Some people believe that an unidentified flying object . . . was somehow involved.

2. Using the information in the article, list the ways that the object Valentich described and the objects people on the ground described were alike and ways that they were different. Write your answers on the lines below.

Similarities

_____

_____

_____

Differences

_____

_____

_____

3. Based on the information in the article, you can predict that

☐ a. the Australian government will continue to search for Frederick Valentich.

☐ b. Frederick Valentich is alive.

☐ c. no one will ever know what happened to Frederick Valentich.

4. Into which of the following theme categories would this story best fit?

☐ a. adventure

☐ b. mystery

☐ c. science fiction

_____ Number of correct answers

Record your personal assessment of your work on the Critical Thinking Chart on page 150.

Personal Response

I can't believe

_____

_____

_____

Self-Assessment

I can't really understand how

_____

_____

_____

Compare and Contrast

Think about the articles you have read in Unit Three. Pick the three articles you thought were the most surprising. Write the titles of the articles in the first column of the chart below. Use information you have learned from the articles to fill in the empty boxes in the chart.

Title	What surprised you in this article?	Describe one of the people in this article.	Would you have liked or disliked this person if you knew him or her? Why?

Which of these stories would you most like to have been in? Why?

_____

_____

Words-per-Minute Table

Unit Three

Directions: If you were timed while reading an article, refer to the Reading Time you recorded in the box at the end of the article. Use this Words-per-Minute Table to determine your reading speed for that article. Then plot your reading speed on the graph on page 148.

Lesson No. of Words	11 1205	12 992	13 1114	14 1011	15 1114	Seconds
1:30	803	661	743	674	743	90
1:40	723	595	668	607	668	100
1:50	657	541	608	551	608	110
2:00	603	496	557	506	557	120
2:10	556	458	514	467	514	130
2:20	516	425	477	433	477	140
2:30	482	397	446	404	446	150
2:40	452	372	418	379	418	160
2:50	425	350	393	357	393	170
3:00	402	331	371	337	371	180
3:10	381	313	352	319	352	190
3:20	362	298	334	303	334	200
3:30	344	283	318	289	318	210
3:40	329	271	304	276	304	220
3:50	314	259	291	264	291	230
4:00	301	248	279	253	279	240
4:10	289	238	267	243	267	250
4:20	278	229	257	233	257	260
4:30	268	220	248	225	248	270
4:40	258	213	239	217	239	280
4:50	249	205	230	209	230	290
5:00	241	198	223	202	223	300
5:10	233	192	216	196	216	310
5:20	226	186	209	190	209	320
5:30	219	180	203	184	203	330
5:40	213	175	197	178	197	340
5:50	207	170	191	173	191	350
6:00	201	165	186	169	186	360
6:10	195	161	181	164	181	370
6:20	190	157	176	160	176	380
6:30	185	153	171	156	171	390
6:40	181	149	167	152	167	400
6:50	176	145	163	148	163	410
7:00	172	142	159	144	159	420
7:10	168	138	155	141	155	430
7:20	164	135	152	138	152	440
7:30	161	132	149	135	149	450
7:40	157	129	145	132	145	460
7:50	154	127	142	129	142	470
8:00	151	124	139	126	139	480

Minutes and Seconds

Plotting Your Progress: Reading Speed

Unit Three

Directions: If you were timed while reading an article, write your words-per-minute rate for that article in the box under the number of the lesson. Then plot your reading speed on the graph by putting a small X on the line directly above the number of the lesson, across from the number of words per minute you read. As you mark your speed for each lesson, graph your progress by drawing a line to connect the X's.

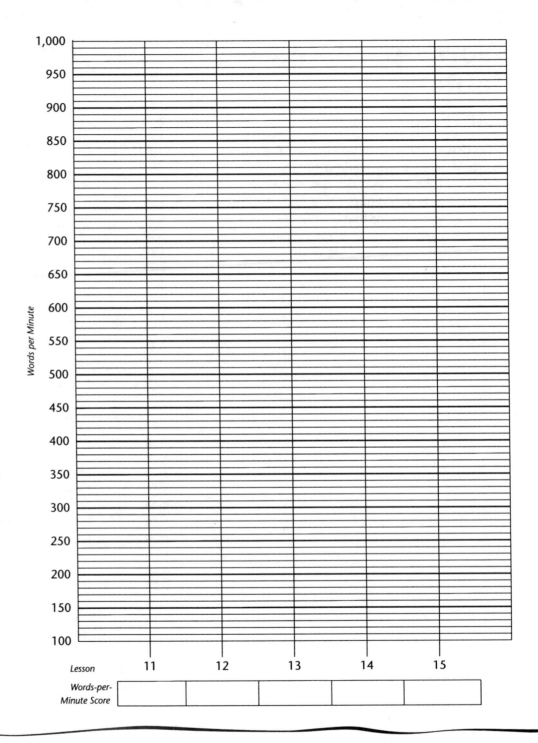

Plotting Your Progress: Reading Comprehension

Unit Three

Directions: Write your Reading Comprehension score for each lesson in the box under the number of the lesson. Then plot your score on the graph by putting a small X on the line directly above the number of the lesson and across from the score you earned. As you mark your score for each lesson, graph your progress by drawing a line to connect the X's.

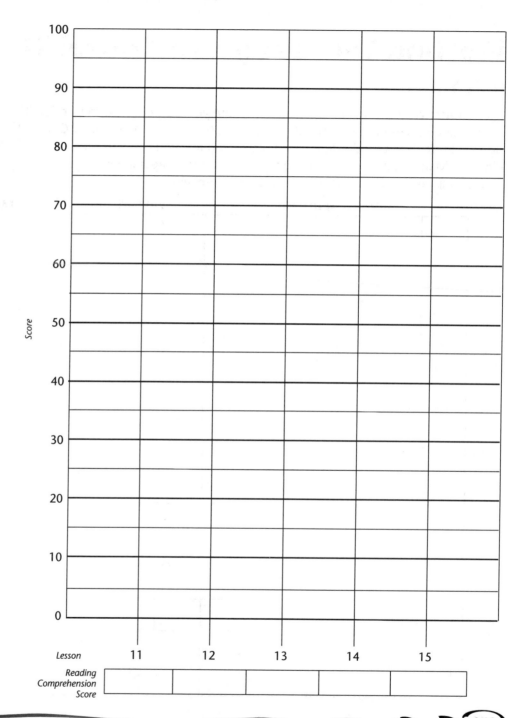

Plotting Your Progress: Critical Thinking

Unit Three

Directions: Work with your teacher to evaluate your responses to the Critical Thinking questions for each lesson. Then fill in the appropriate spaces in the chart below. For each lesson and each type of Critical Thinking question, do the following: Mark a minus sign (–) in the box to indicate areas in which you feel you could improve. Mark a plus sign (+) to indicate areas in which you feel you did well. Mark a minus-slash-plus sign (–/+) to indicate areas in which you had mixed success. Then write any comments you have about your performance, including ideas for improvement.

Lesson	Author's Approach	Summarizing and Paraphrasing	Critical Thinking
11			
12			
13			
14			
15			

Photo Credits